T0285119

"The tragic murde
of his girlfriend on an
January of 1957 is by a
dents of southeast Miss
forgotten, or never know

"But Dan Joslyn, of Tu
lugen's Charleston, Missou
bers. And he has revisited
interviews, court records, a
ing and insightful account o
just wanted a few dollars on a
nificant social, racial, criminal
consequences. This is a sober a
ior in southeast Missouri in the

--**Dr. Frank Nickell,** emeritu
History, Southeast Missouri State
the Historical Society of Missouri

"Dan Joslyn has given us a chillin
school youth, Johnny Malugen, and
Set in Southeast Missouri during the
and the civil rights movement, fear rise
and white communities. Joslyn describe
seeking to solve the murder and rape. Th
testimonies, makes a valuable contributic
literature."

--**Reverend James D. Yoder, Ph.D.,** Au
*Tears, and Boil and Bubble: The Amazon Wome*

# The Murder of Johnny Malugen

## A True Story of Race, Violence and Hope in a Southern Town

Dan Joslyn

Joslyn, Wallace Danforth, 1939, - author.
The murder of Johnny Malugen: a true story of race, violence and hope in a southern town /Dan Joslyn
Tulsa, OK Dan Joslyn, 2021.| includes 18 b&w photographs, includes index
ISBN 9780578867465 (hardcover) |ISBN 9780578-867472 (ebook)
LCSH: Malugen, John Robert, 1938-1957. | Castleberry, June, 1938 – 1997. African Americans – Missouri – History. | Crime – Missouri – History - 20th century. | Murder -Missouri – Case studies. | Missouri - Race relations. | BISAC: HISTORY / United States/ State & Local/Midwest (IA, IL, IN, KS, MI, MN, MO, ND, NE, OH, SD, WI). | SOCIAL SCIENCE/ Race & Ethnic Relations. | TRUE CRIME / Murder / General.
Classification: LCC 472.M55 j67 2021 |DCC 977.8983 j

Book design and typesetting by Charles Michael Levy

Cover design by Jim Schroeder

Printed by Sheridan

We, as human beings, must be willing to accept people
who are different from ourselves.

*Barbara Jordan*

To

The Malugen Family

*Erma*

*Joan*

*Jim*

*Johnny*

*"Junior"*

*Warren*

*Wayne*

Who have suffered great loss

and

*Mable Bradford*

*Louis Craft*

*Leatha Crenshaw*

*Willie Curtis*

*Katie Davis*

*Adam Holman*

*Pat Montjoy*

*Jerome Price*

Who stood firm.

# Contents

# Preface

This is a true story, not a novel, not fiction, not historical fiction, not based on a true story. It *is* a true story. It is history.

The information contained in this book came from many newspaper accounts, 45 personal interviews, and official documents from the State of Missouri. Because I was a classmate of Johnny Malugen at Charleston High School, I witnessed some of the events described in this book.

For years I had thought someone should write a book about these events, but no one did. So I wrote it myself. Dr. Frank Nickell, a retired history professor at Southeast Missouri State University, said, "In another 20 years nobody will be living who remembers these events, and the myth will have outgrown the facts." This is a record of the facts.

If you, the reader, are perplexed by something in the text, you might find something in the endnotes that explains it.

# Acknowledgments

I thank Dr. Frank Nickell, emeritus Assistant Director of the State Historical Society of Missouri, emeritus Director of the Center for Regional History (of Southeast Missouri), and emeritus history professor at Southeast Missouri State University for his encouragement and guidance in the writing of this book. Without him, this book would never have seen the light of day. I had written a good book before, but Dr. Nickell's guidance raised the writing of this book to a new level. I thank the late "Liz" Wallhausen Anderson, former editor of the Charleston *Enterprise-Courier,* for leading me to Dr. Nickell.

Partway through this book, my writing skills had reached their limit, and I was beginning to "miss the forest for the trees." My wife, Moreen, an excellent writer, sat down with me for some hard work and made this a better book. She suggested numerous revisions, both major and minor. We argued some, but she stuck to her guns and almost always convinced me that she was right. I owe her a great debt.

Betsey Bruner, retired writer for the *Arizona Daily Sun,* lent her professional editing and writing skills to improving the clarity and readability of the book.

The *Enterprise-Courier* and *The Daily Sikeston Standard* provided thorough and detailed accounts of the events related to the murder of Johnny Malugen. Without the back issues of these newspapers, it would have been impossible for me to obtain all the facts and facets in this case, much less to put them in their proper order. "Liz" Anderson retrieved the relevant issues from the *Enterprise-Courier,* and Norma Faye O'Connell found a great many articles from *The Daily Sikeston Standard* and obtained court records relevant to the crimes committed. Sharon Sanders, librarian/ historian of the *Southeast Missourian,* found any information I requested in short order. Deborah Gunter, Recording Secretary of the Scott County Historical Center in Benton, Missouri shared with me what she knew about the Malugen murder and guided me to the *Chaffee Signal* as an additional source of information. I thank the *Chaffee Signal* for giving me access to its back issues. I also thank First Lady Betty Hearnes for leading me to the Missouri Department of Corrections for more information.

Art Wallhausen and Dr. Charles Michael Levy kindly read the entire manuscript and provided editorial advice and suggestions. Art was kind enough to write a comprehensive endorsement for the back cover.

I thank Sheridan for treating me like a prince and doing a beautiful job of printing this book and another in 2004.

I greatly appreciate the willingness of Johnny Malugen's brother, Rev. Jim Malugen, his sister, Erma Malugen Vaughn, and his niece, Diane LaCroix for sharing their memories of Johnny.

The final design for the book cover was created by painter, graphic designer, and photographer Jim Schroeder of Flagstaff, Arizona. I thank professional artist Carolyn Curry for her preliminary work on the cover design and artwork. Glenda Manche and Dessie Gross lent their artistic talent using an idea of mine which turned out to be not a good idea.

But they did their best.

Charleston Downtown
Main Street 1955

Charleston High School 1983

**Early 1950's**
**The Famous Johnnies Drive Inn**
**Hwy 60 East**

**The Russell Hotel**
**February 28, 1948**

# Introduction

I grew up in the "Missouri Bootheel" in the southeast corner of the state. This is an area seldom thought of when an image of "The South" emerges. But, when and where I grew up was Southern in culture. It was "cotton country" before the modern Civil Rights era began. For African Americans the "rules" were those of "Jim Crow" in which custom and the legal system restricted the freedoms and opportunities for our black population. I had just turned fifteen, when in 1954 the Supreme Court of the United States ruled that "separate but equal" schools were unconstitutional.

When I was young, I was acquainted with very few African Americans. The first black person I knew was Bud Johnson who worked many years for my grandparents and lived in a small one-room house behind their house. Our family lived next door to my grandparents, and when I was a toddler, Bud sometimes looked after me. I spent considerable time with him. My mother once told me not to say "ain't" because it wasn't a word, but Bud had taught it to me and I didn't see anything wrong with it.

When I was older, I asked Bud, "Who was the worst kid, me or my father?" Bud said, "He was the worst kid." Later on, Bud moved to "colored town" to be with "his people." I was told that he had "gotten old and cranky."

Before I started school, a black woman named May looked after me for a while. She was young and pretty, and I wanted her to stay with us a long time. She said she would but disappointed me by leaving after a short time.

Sometime after May left, Lilly B. Phillips came to cook our noon meal. My mother would pick her up in the morning and bring her to our house. Lilly B. was older than May but younger than Bud. In the summer, I often got up at five in the morning, went fishing, and brought home a string of catfish for Lilly B. to cook for lunch. After we had eaten our lunch and Lilly B. had eaten hers, my mother drove her back to her house. She lived in a small unpainted house on a dirt road with her blind brother, Buddy. After a heavy rain her road was hard to navigate.

Lilly B. was with us a good many years. I remember my mother being disturbed about how Lilly B. was treated at the Post Office. She had taken a package to be mailed but was told that it wasn't wrapped well enough. She went home, wrapped it again, and came back, only to be turned away again. After she had wrapped it a third time, it was mailed.

Lilly B. eventually became old, tired, and stiff. When she died, my mother and I went to her funeral.

Pauline Moore and Odell Wadkins, Jr. were unforgettable individuals. When I first saw Pauline, she was washing one of our dogs in a cast iron kettle, wearing a dress, beads, and a large hat. I remember her throwing a stick for the dog to retrieve and laughing delightfully every time the dog brought it back. One day I was sitting at the kitchen table with Pauline while she was eating her lunch. This was in the mid 1950s, and there was already talk about a man going to the moon. Pauline said, "Nobody'll ever do that because you can't get by Jesus! Just look at the moon when you're walking. You can't get by it. It just keep walking along beside you. You can't get by Jesus." In another conversation, Pauline said she could remember when Abraham Lincoln "was in." I told Lilly B. that Pauline said she could remember when Abraham Lincoln was president. Lilly B. said, "I can't, but Buddy can."

The Great Depression of the 1930s was hard on everyone but especially on African Americans because they were so poor to begin with. In those days most black children didn't have the means or opportunity to go past the first few years of grade school. They had to work in the fields during the growing and harvest seasons and at home during the winter. Pauline told my father that during the depression she had raised two piglets as pets, but when they were big enough she had to slaughter them for food. She said, "It was just like killing my own kids, but we had to stay alive."

Odell Wadkins, all around handyman, helped with my father's bird dogs, and after "Uncle" Gene Howard died, Odell also took care of his game chickens. Odell was always friendly and good humored. If he accidentally let a rooster out of its pen or slipped up some way, my father would chew him out royally. Odell would cheerfully agree with whatever shortcomings my father had accused him of.

It was no secret that Odell drank heavily, even resorting to wood alcohol when "necessary." He said that every Saturday he spent the night in "Old Cairo," which was what he called the jail. It gave him a place to sleep and sober up. Among his many talents, Odell, who was toothless, could eat most anything including steak. I was amazed to learn that he could chew poison ivy with no ill effects. He also had an eagle eye for four leaf clovers.

Odell was often around when I did my chores. My father would pay me a penny for every six "duck greens" I dug up in the yard. One day I earned an entire dollar and remember Odell sitting with me and helping count out 600 duck greens from the wire basket I used to collect them in.

When I was in high school, Odell told me that he had 15 children from a good many women, and he knew each one and where they lived. Odell was well traveled for a black man in the South during the 1950s. He would pick cherries every summer in Michigan but said he had to stay up all night to keep someone from stealing his money.

The last time I saw Odell was in 1979 when I was 40 years old. He was sitting on a porch at the dump with Lizzie, his latest girlfriend. He had gone blind from drinking wood alcohol, and I will never forget Odell's blind eyes looking up at me from that old gray, broken-down porch. He died two months later.

On May 17, 1954, the Supreme Court of the United States ruled unanimously that race-based segregation of children into separate public schools violated he Equal Protection Clause of the Fourteenth Amendment of the United States Constitution. The preponderance of evidence was judged to be that the schools were *not* equal. This decision would make it illegal for school systems to deny an education to students based on race. The *implementation* of this court decision, however, was left to lower federal courts and other administrative entities such as school boards. This would prove difficult and take a very long time.[1]

There were several standoffs between those given the responsibility to enforce the Supreme Court's decision and those opposing it. In the fall of 1957, Governor Orval Faubus of Arkansas ordered the Arkansas National Guard to block nine black students from entering Central High School in Little Rock. In response, President Eisenhower ordered the 101st Airborne Division of the Army to escort the students into the school.[2]

In 1962, Governor Ross Barnett attempted to prevent James Meredith from entering the University of Mississippi. Meredith entered the university but not without the intervention of 500 U.S. Marshals and an Army combat division from Ft. Campbell, Kentucky. During the confrontation two people were killed. Despite intense harassment, Meredith graduated from the University of Mississippi and later earned a law degree from Columbia University in New York City.[3,4]

In 1963, Governor George Wallace attempted to block two black students from enrolling at the University of Alabama, ostensibly to keep his promise made in his inaugural speech, "segregation today, segregation tomorrow, segregation forever." President Kennedy nationalized the Alabama National Guard, and Governor Wallace stepped aside.[5]

These headline grabbing confrontations, however, did not report all events related to school desegregation. The very first school system to be desegregated was that of Charleston, Arkansas, 20 miles east of Ft. Smith. Their school board, on July 27, 1954, two and a half months after the Supreme Court decision, voted unanimously to desegregate their entire school system. They had obtained promises from local officials, business leaders, and the newspaper not to discuss their plans with any outside source. This decision likely avoided conflict and the process went smoothly[6].

Surprisingly, another Charleston school system followed suit a year later. In September 1955, when eight black students enrolled in Charleston High School in Charleston, *Missouri,* about 300 miles northeast of Charleston, Arkansas[5]. The desegregation of Charleston High School appeared to be progressing smoothly until the murder of Johnny Malugen.

Endnotes

1. Dudley, M. E. *Brown v. Board of Education* (1954) New York: Twenty-First Century Books, 1995

2. Orval Eugene Faubus (1910-1994) www.spartacus-educational.com

3. James Meredith Biography & Facts HISTORY

4. Meredtith, James. *Three Years in Mississippi* University Press of Mississippi, 2019

5. *George Wallace: American Populist* by Stephan Lesher. Addison-Wesley Publishing Company, 1994. ISBN 0-201-62210-6

6. Desegregation of Charleston Schools – Encyclopedia of Arkansas *of arkansas.net/encylopedia/entry-detail.aspx?entryID=730–accessed January 9, 2019*

# Part 1: Before 1957

## 1

## Johnny Malugen

In 1957, there were 350 students in the Charleston Missouri High School, and everyone there knew John Robert Malugen. Johnny was a teammate of mine on the track team and the most popular boy in the school, handsome, square jaw, blue eyes, and thick coarse sandy-brown hair. A few of the boys were jealous of his good looks and winning ways with the girls, but nobody disliked him.[1] He was quiet and soft-spoken, but friendly with everyone. Despite being a star running back and co-captain of the football team, he had, according to a friend, "no high and mighty football player attitude."[2] One of his teammates said, "Johnny was a jolly, fun loving guy, and I enjoyed being around him. He was relaxed, and I never saw him mad."[3]

Shortly before Johnny began high school, his parents moved to Potosi, Missouri, about 130 miles northwest of Charleston. Johnny, however, wanted to stay in Charleston and play football. His sister, Erma, who had married and was still in Charleston, invited him to stay with her family. However, because Erma and her husband's house was not yet finished, Johnny spent his first year in high school with the family of Jack Powell, whose son, Arlen, was one of Johnny's teammates.[4]

After Johnny moved in with his sister and brother-in-law, Erma said that "Johnny was very good about baby-sitting our children even though he was very busy with school, athletics, working, and girls. With all these activities, he was so worn out at the end of the day that he slept very soundly at night. In the morning we had to pour cold water on his face to wake him up for school.[5]"

Johnny's pride and joy was his stick shift, V-8, '49 Mercury coupe. It had flush-body fender skirts, white wall tires, and was a dark navy blue, so dark it looked almost purple. Johnny kept it in perfect condition. He worked at Ferrell's Grocery Store down by the old depot to earn enough money to make the payments.[6] He had it 'souped up' with a muffler and chrome extension that made the tail-pipe easy to spot, and if the girls didn't see it, they heard it. It was a chick car with a James Dean look.[7]

In addition to school, athletics, working, and girls, Johnny found time for a little mischief. Paul Hill, one of his teammates, said, "One morning before school, Johnny and me shared a six-pack of Pabst Blue Ribbon for breakfast. We got it at Renfro's in Badland.[8] We were underage, and that was the only place we could get it. Even if there were blacks in the store, Mr. Renfro would serve us first because we were high school kids and he wanted us out of there as fast as possible. You never knew when the police would show up. After we drank the beer, we went to school, got through our classes OK, and then went to football practice. On one play, Johnny got tackled with a hard hit to the stomach and went to the sidelines. When Johnny started throwing up, Dee Bonner, the coach, slowly walked over to him, smelled the stale beer on his breath, and said, 'Well, was it worth it?'"[9]

## Endnotes

1. Bob Carlisle, Interview by author, 2002
2. Eleanor Switzer Moxley, Interview by author, 2004
3. Kenneth Weakley, Interview by author, July 7, 2010
4. Rev. Jim Malugen, Interview by author, August 9, 2003
5. Erma Malugen Vaughn, Interview by author, April 3, 2010
6. Rev. Jim Malugen, Interview by author, August 9, 2003
7. Paul Hill, Interview by author, August 18, 2003
8. "Badland" referred to the black or "colored" part of town and sometimes to an area in this part of town with night clubs and bars where there were often fights on Saturday nights. "Colored Town" was the polite way to refer to that part of town. "Black" was not in fashion at that time.
9. Paul Hill, Interview by author, August 18, 2003

# 2

# A Small Southern Town

Charleston is a town of 5,000[1] in the southeast corner of Missouri, 14 miles from the confluence of the Ohio and Mississippi rivers and within 50 miles of four states: Illinois, Kentucky, Tennessee, and Arkansas. Charleston, in Mississippi County, is in the Missouri Bootheel, a thumb poking down into Arkansas, and part of an alluvial plain deposited eons ago by the Mississippi River. Some say that "Ole Man River" quietly stole the rich farmland from the Yankees.

I grew up there in the 1940s and 1950s when the pace of life was slower: no freeways, shopping malls, or fast food restaurants. People took time to know their neighbors, their neighbors' children, and often their neighbors' dogs. The families on our street were rich, poor, and in between. Nobody had ever heard of a gated community.

Charleston people were not city folks. After World War II, business in downtown Charleston picked up markedly, and for a time the population approached 6,000. To accommodate the traffic, the city put in parking meters and required diagonal parking along the entire three blocks of downtown. One afternoon, Judy Gallagher, a high school student, was putting a dime in the meter when a friend walked by and greeted her. Judy went into Brewer & Trickey's drug store, got what she wanted, came out, and got back in her car. Fifteen minutes later, her friend came by again and said, "Judy, why have you been sitting there so long?" Judy said, "I'm waiting for the meter to run out so I can leave."[2]

In those days, there were no leash laws, and dogs were free to roam but usually stayed in their own neighborhoods. Our water spaniel, Patsy, however, would trot four or five blocks to the grade school where the children knew her and didn't mind her drinking from the water fountains. We gave one of Patsy's puppies to Odell Wadkins, the African American man who took care of my father's game chickens. He was a preacher's son and named the puppy Shadrach, Meshach and Abednego. Shadrach, Meshach, and Abednego were Biblical characters who were put in a fiery furnace because they would not abandon their faith. As often as not, dogs were given people's names. Our bird dogs were Jason, David, Betty, Bruce, Jimmy. and Tony. Our coon hound was Honus, named after Honus Wagner, the baseball player. Honus did more than just chase raccoons uptrees. In those days, our milk was delivered to our house in glass quart bottles by the milkman on a horse drawn wagon. One day a bottle got cracked and leaked milk all over the kitchen floor. Honus was invited in and quickly lapped it up. In contrast to dogs having people's names, many grown men were known by nicknames that could have worked as well for dogs: Puffy, Poochy, Peachy, Joker, Bad Eye, Baby Red, and Bologna Dog. I never knew these men by any other names. We had no video games or computers, preferred to be outdoors and got a lot of exercise. We took long hikes, crawled around in a barn full of fresh hay, played softball or football in a neighbor's yard, or swam in the public pool and sometimes a pond. On summer evenings, we played games such as "Mother May I" or "Red Rover, Red Rover." We fished, hunted game, and a few of us, very few, caught water snakes along a ditch bank and took them home.

In the summer, a favorite place for kids to spend time was Hequembourg's Pond. It was owned by Frank Hequembourg whom we called "Uncle Frankie." Uncle Frankie entertained us with imaginative tales and admonitions, never letting the facts get in the way of a good story. For example, the remnants of an old chimney that stood by his pond was "left from a house that had belonged to Davy Crockett's sister." The giant alligator snapping turtle "lurking in the mud on the bottom of the pond, half starved," was just waiting for a chance to bite off the arm or leg of a kid. We never doubted the reality of this turtle, but looking back, I suspect Uncle Frankie "kept it down there" to remind us kids that swimming in the pond was forbidden. One night I dreamed that the evil beast, bigger than a Buffalo, crawled out of the pond and chased me all the way home, right down the middle of State Street!

Uncle Frankie had three dogs, Jick, Jack, and Jill. He sometimes dressed Jill in a dress and sunbonnet, Jack and Jick in shorts and T-shirts, and put Jill in a baby carriage. He taught Jack and Jick to stand on their hindlegs with their front paws on the handle of the carriage and push it around town with Jill in it. One day, Uncle Frankie let Carol Yates and me supervise the dogs all by ourselves.

We felt proud, important, and responsible as we guided them around town.[3]

* * *

In those days there were fewer opportunities for kids to get into trouble. There were no drugs, no gangs, and very little crime. For that reason, parents could give their children more freedom and only expected them to keep their mischief within bounds. The children, however, were not angels, and the hot, humid summer afternoons and warm, quiet evenings bred just enough boredom to stimulate their imaginations.

On Saturday nights there was dancing in the basement of the Russell Hotel where a window fan opened into the alley and provided a way for us to pepper the dancers with our bean shooters.

One night, during the annual fair at the Catholic Church, while everyone was distracted by the cake walk, several children rescued the competitors in the turtle races. We put them in my homemade go cart and took them to Uncle Frankie's pond to spare them from becoming turtle soup.

Our house was three blocks from the water tower, and on several occasions, I shot the tank with a .22 caliber rifle from my bedroom window. Paul Hill stood under the tower to see if he could hear the sound of lead hitting the steel tank. Paul's version of this story is that we shot it from the roof so my mother wouldn't catch us, but I remember the hole in the window screen.

When mischief did exceed tolerable limits, parents usually dealt with it without involving the police. Between the eighth and ninth grades, Paul Lee Moore and I would steal fishing plugs from the H & H Hardware and sell them at Teen Town for a third of their retail price. We thought we were big shots until the owner of the store caught us red handed and called our mothers. I spent the longest week in my life waiting for my father to return from a business trip and deal with me. The fear and turmoil I suffered that week was punishment enough, and when I was finally forced to face my father I was already crying and "quivering in my boots." Dad said, "I don't care what you did, just quit that blubbering. Go talk to Grandma." Since then, I haven't stolen anything and seldom lied.

* * *

We didn't spend all our time playing and getting into mischief. We went to school. In my generation and that of my father, born in 1907, the best remembered teacher in Charleston was Miss Mattie Henry. She was the seventh and eighth grade writing and grammar teacher at the Eugene Field School. Miss Mattie began teaching when she was 14 years old in one-room schoolhouses in the country. After she came to town, she taught some three generations of seventh and eighth grade students. Some said she was the best teacher they ever had, and others, including the author, thought she was the worst. Either way, all of us have crystal clear memories of the way Miss Mattie kept her students in line. To maintain discipline, Miss Mattie employed her temper, her paddle, and her fist, often coming up behind an errant boy and hitting him between the shoulder blades. The girls were generally better behaved and got along peaceably with Miss Henry. Eleanor Switzer, whose classroom conduct was impeccable, told me, "Miss Mattie often beat on the boy who sat behind me, and I was afraid she would miss and hit me!"[4]

Miss Mattie's appearance was formidable. She was of sturdy build with a large, square head, and expressive eyes, one brown and one blue. After Miss Mattie retired, some of her former students would visit her and found her to be a welcoming and friendly hostess, not at all like the woman they remembered from the classroom. She once told me, "Sometimes they ask me to substitute, and I tell them, 'Fine, but don't forget, I paddle!'" I think Miss Mattie genuinely believed she knew the right way to discipline children and just wouldn't backdown.

* * *

Race relations in the six or seven counties in the Bootheel during the 1940s and 1950s were succinctly summarized in Dan Whittle's book, *Canalou: People, Culture, Bootheel Town,* published in 2013. Canalou is a very small town about 25 miles southwest of Charleston. Whittle wrote:

"Bigotry is a subject folks don't like thinking about, but it was part of the fabric of life in the Bootheel region's culture of southeast Missouri where I grew up in the 1940's and 1950s.

"A lot of Americans don't realize that Missouri has Deep South Delta-style farming country along the Mississippi River, much like that in the state of Mississippi. And we had social morals similar to Deep South's culture.[5]

"Was I reared a racial bigot?

"Yes

"Did I know I was a bigot as a boy?

"No, for our elders taught us that was the way things were ordered to be.

"Some Southern Baptist preachers used Bible verses telling us the races were not equal and should not mix."[6]

* * *

Julia Garry moved from a small Mississippi County farm to Charleston in 1950 when she was twelve years old. Her memories of farm life are happy ones. "When we lived in the country; we loved to feed the hogs and milk the cows. We got excited about it. When we milked, we would squirt each other, aiming for wide open mouths."

Julia recalls, "When we moved to town, we learned what we black children could and couldn't do. We just stayed in our own neighborhoods and didn't think much about it. If we wanted to go to the movies we knew where to sit. We didn't need to be reminded that we couldn't eat at Johnny's Drive-in where they would refuse to serve us."

Julia remembers that in grade school, every day before class began, the teacher said an opening prayer, and each child recited a Bible verse. She recalls a field trip to Memphis to a fair during the only week it was open to black people. "At home we did 'tom walking' on tin cans. We would punch a hole in either side of two tin cans, put a string through the holes, and tie the string to a handle. We would pull up on the string to keep the cans on our feet as we walked and raced each other to see who got to the finish line first. We played hide-and-seek outdoors in the summer and indoors in the winter. We liked outdoors better because there were more places to hide. We also liked to play tricks on each other. A piece of rubber hose put in just the right place can be as frightening as a *real* snake! We never had "sleep overs" because our houses weren't big enough for extra kids."

"When they began integrating the high school, I didn't want to go. If they didn't want me, I didn't want to be there, so I moved to Joliet, lived with my brother, and finished school there. I liked my teenage years and enjoyed school." Julia said she felt it was much more difficult for girls to finish school now than when she was growing up.[7]

Deborah Betts Turner was one of 16 children, the daughter of a minister. Debbie graduated from the segregated Lincoln High School a year or two before I graduated from Charleston High School. She said, "I had a good childhood. Our parents protected us, and we couldn't just get up and go running off to someone else's house without asking our father. If he wasn't home, we asked our mother. We got three hot meals a day and a snack at bedtime if we wanted. We didn't deal with white children at all because we lived in a different part of town. That was neither good nor bad."[8]

Like Julia Garry, Ruth Boyd moved from the country to Charleston when she was twelve years old. She recalls, "Our parents pretty much shielded us from prejudice. The first I remember considering it was when I was in the ninth or tenth grade and wondered why our books looked so old and worn. I decided they must have been 'hand me downs' from the white schools."

"My parents were too proud to get commodities, so it was hard to get enough to eat. I was skinny. There was a 'green patch' near our house, and the whole neighborhood lived off it for a whole winter. There always seemed to be turnip greens to pick, and sometimes we'd pull the roots and all. And there were other things in the 'green patch' besides turnip greens. I remember too, Dr. Rolwing letting us pick up corn from his field after it was harvested. We'd pick enough to sell to the grain elevator and have money to buy food for a week.

"After we moved to Charleston, we'd fill a cattle trough with the pump and swim in it. If we didn't have a swimming suit, we swam in our clothes. "There was a place attached to the Currin Cafe where we could dance to records, and we danced with both boys and girls. We also went to 'Sweetheart Hops' at the school gym. We could see cowboy movies for a nickel or a dime at the Haynes Entertainment Hall, but we always had to be home by ten o'clock, and that meant *home,* not on the way. There wasn't as much violence then as there is today.

"As a teenager, I worked four hours a day for a lady, but when cotton picking time came, I told her I had to quit because it paid more. She said she'd pay me whatever I could make picking cotton.

"When we lived in the country near Drinkwater Sewer, we would do'tom walking' on tin cans. We swam in a shallow stream, and if we were small enough, we we'd get in a tire and roll down a hill. When we moved closer to town, we would skate on Fish Lake when it froze. We skated on our shoes because we didn't have ice skates and were pretty good at it. We liked to play 'pop the whip.' We'd hold hands, the leader would run fast and then make a sharp turn. The last one would usually fall down, and nobody wanted to be on the end of the whip.

"We made our own toys. One was made from an empty spool. We'd put a skinny stick through it and spin it. The spool was marked, so we could see which part faced up. We'd 'put up' pecans and sometimes peppermints and could win or lose them depending on which mark faced up when it stopped.

"I enjoyed living in town better than the country because I had more friends. Up to a point, I thought Charleston was a pleasant place to grow up, but always wanted to leave and did, right after high school."[9]

Endnotes

1. As of 2018 the population of Charleston was technically 6,000 because a prison had been built there. Without the prison the population was 5,000.

2. Mildred Reeves Burnett. Interview by author, 2010

3. Bud and Don Hequembourg helped the author flesh out his memories of the three dogs during interviews by the author on January 8, 2013

4. Eleanor Switzer Moxley, Interview by author, November 21, 2010

5. According to Boyd Allen of Quora, an internet site, "Missouri is generally midwestern at the top, and progressively more southern as you head south. This applies not only to accents, but politics, religion, and number of Confederate flags per capita." As of September 8, 2018 the author was unable to retrieve the source of this quote. He had found it before on Google.

6. Whittle, Dan. *Canalou: People, Culture, Bootheel Town.* Southeast Missouri State University Press, 2013, page 408

7. Julia Garry, Interviews by author, June 6, 2012; June 18, 2012; & June 19, 2012

8. Deborah Betts Turner, Interview by author, August 21, 2012

9. Ruth Boyd, Interview by author, June 19, 2012

# 3

# Desegregation of Charleston High School[1]

I was sitting in our front yard on a summer afternoon in 1955 pondering the news that our high school was to be desegregated that fall. A Southern thought pattern, typical of the time, entered my head: "We're going to have to get together and do something about this." I got up, walked over to the Japanese magnolia, did a few chin ups, and forgot all about it.

When I began my junior year that fall, I had eight black[2] schoolmates: Willie Curtis, Pat Montjoy, Mable Bradford, Louis Craft, Leatha Crenshaw, Jerome Price, Adam Holman, and Maudine Brent. Jerome and Adam were seniors, a year ahead of me. Maudine Brent moved to California before the end of the semester, leaving seven black students in the school.[3] Every one of them was courteous and respectful of both their classmates and teachers. It never occurred to me to object to their presence.

**Willie Curtis** was a serious student who had transferred from a segregated school in Mississippi to the newly desegregated

Charleston High School in hopes of a better education. He had family in Charleston and had lived there before.

**Pat Montjoy**, petite and studious, came from a family of educators and land owners. Her extended family owned a good portion of land on Wolf Island, south and east of Charleston. One of her Montjoy ancestors, Louis Montjoy, had come to Wolf Island in 1865 with only a team of mules. He eventually accumulated 600 acres of good land which he passed down to his heirs.[4] As the heirs multiplied, many of them sold their portions to Pat's uncle, L.V. Montjoy. At one time there was a place on Wolf Island known as Montjoy Corner.[5]

Although Pat was studious, she also liked to have fun. One student, Shirley Cossey, told me, "I remember cutting up with Pat and June Hillhouse in Miss Miles's civics class when Miss Miles was out of the room."[6]

**Louis Craft** was a quiet, hard working student who could get along with most anyone. He was tall, well coordinated and solid, a good basketball player.

**Leatha Crenshaw** was from Wyatt, a small town seven miles east of Charleston. There was no school for black children in Wyatt, so they were forced to take their schooling in a church. Leatha's mother, along with five other mothers, had tried to enroll their children in the white grade school even though they knew they would be refused. However, by the time Leatha was ready for seventh grade, an elementary school for black children *had* been built, so Leatha attended seventh and eighth grades in the new school. Because there was no high school in Wyatt, all students, both black and white, went to Charleston. The white students went to Charleston High School whereas the black students went to the segregated Lincoln School. Leatha completed her first two years of high school at the Lincoln School, then transferred to Charleston High School as soon as it was desegregated.[7]

**Mable Bradford** was a quiet student and did very well academically. Her family, like Pat Montjoy's, were educators and high achievers.

Many years after our graduation from Charleston High School, Mable shared with me some memories of her first day there. She said that on that day, she and the other black students rode to the school in taxi cabs, and that local black leaders, clergy, and members of the NAACP rode with them. "On the way," she said, "I saw many lovely homes, a real contrast to the part of town where my black classmates and I lived. This school had always been segregated - until that day." Upon arrival the students got out of the cabs and the police led them to the front of the school. She said, "I hadn't seen so many white people in one place in my life!"

Mable wrote, "Fear follows us along as we walk through the tunnel formed by the surrounding mob. I'm afraid. This seems like a dream, but my eyes and ears tell me it's real. Words swirl around my head; I wonder what a 'nigger' is. I was raised as a proud American Negro from a family of educated teachers. My brother is a CPA, the first black person to work for the IRS; he was appointed by Senator Jacob Javits of New York."

As Mable and her classmates entered the school, the principal, the teachers, and some of the students greeted them. "Safe inside," Mable thought, "I know that my Lord Jesus is with us." She found her home room teacher to be very supportive, a mature woman who took no nonsense. Mable said, "As the semester progressed, the teachers were fair and treated us black students according to our behavior and participation in class."

Mable said her civics teacher was a compassionate white man from Arkansas. He let Mable, Pat, one black boy, and one white boy eat lunch in his classroom every day. Mable felt like he was their own personal counselor and helped them work through their hurt. [8]

**Adam Holman** was one of 12 children born to a sharecropping family in Mississippi County. He said, "My father was not educated but had a lot of common sense and wouldn't go along with anything he thought was wrong. He participated in the 1939 Sharecropper's Strike."[9] The strike occurred after white landowners, to their financial advantage, evicted sharecroppers, both black and white, from their houses in the middle of winter.[10] Adam was a year old when his family was evicted.

Adam said, "Coach Bonner protected Jerome and me when we got to Charleston High School. If there was any trouble, we told Coach Bonner, and he straightened it out, not just on the basketball team but any kind of trouble. The principal, Mr. Williams, respected Bonner and made sure the teachers treated Jerome and me right. We didn't have any trouble with the teachers at all."[11]

Adam and Jerome Price entered Charleston High as seniors. Adam was modest, relaxed, and friendly; Jerome was confident, polite, and socially skilled. As far as I could tell, they got along well with their teachers and with their classmates, both black or white. As talented athletes, they contributed a great deal to the competitiveness of the basketball team. They were also fast runners and record setting high jumpers on the track team.

**Jerome Price** was raised by his paternal grandmother in Charleston and attended the all black Lincoln School through his junior year. While a student at the Lincoln School, he and Pat Young were selected Homecoming King and Queen. Jerome said, "People thought we were a couple, and I just let them think that. She was good looking. Pat Young, Pat Montjoy, and I are cousins." Jerome's mother lived in Chicago, and he had planned to finish high school there, but the NAACP, of which he was a member, wanted him to help desegregate Charleston High School. That wasn't his preference, but he chose to cooperate. Jerome remembers stopping with the track team on the way back from a meet and being denied entrance to a restaurant. He and Adam were told to go to the back door and pick up their food. A white member of the team offered to stand up for them, but Jerome said, "We appreciate your kindness, but this is not your problem, it's ours." He and Adam went back to the bus without their meals. [12]

**Katie Davis** and Teresa Jones began Charleston High School in 1956 as juniors, a year after the other black students did. Teresa Jones moved to Detroit after her first semester. Leatha Crenshaw said. "Katie was feisty and didn't take things sitting down. If anybody called her 'Congo Katie' they had her to deal with." Some students called Louis Craft "Congo Louie." Katie graduated in 1958.

I did not witness firsthand any conflicts between white and black students during the first three semesters following desegregation, but that doesn't mean they didn't happen.

Because I found our black students to be friendly, polite, and talented, I had assumed they had been hand-picked by the NAACP. Years later, however, I asked Leatha Crenshaw about this. She said

"No, our parents were achievers and wanted us to have a better education. The only way the NAACP could have been involved would have been indirectly through Mrs. Helen Currin who was a prominent black leader in Charleston and heavily involved with the NAACP. She may have influenced our parents, but they made their own decisions."[13]

Beginning in the late 1980s, some white students began transferring from Charleston High School to schools that were almost all white, such as East Prairie, Kelly Public Schools in Scott County, or Notre Dame in Cape Girardeau. In some cases, this was a matter of racial preference but by no means the only reason. Some schools had better athletic and sports programs and some, such as Notre Dame, had higher academic standards. At Notre Dame, a private school, parents had not only to give permission but also pay tuition and most likely textbooks which were very expensive. To live in Charleston and go to Notre Dame would require a round trip almost every weekday of 70 miles.

At the present time, 2020, most of the white students in Charleston have transferred to other schools whereas most black students have remained in Charleston. Unfortunately, he majority of black families do not have the resources to send their children elsewhere. As mentioned above, there are many reasons affecting decisions of whether to go or stay.[14],[15]

## Endnotes

1. For more information about the desegregation of Charleston High School, see *Historical Context: 1950-2000* at the end of the book.

2. A word about the terms "African American," "Black," "Negro," and "Colored:" I understand that people prefer different terms depending on their age, background, and other influences. When I was growing up, the African American part of Charleston was called "Colored Town," and black people were often called "Coloreds." Another term, unfortunately, was the N-word. Although currently outmoded, the "CP" in NAACP stood for "Colored People" and still does. In formal writing such as newspapers and magazines, "Negro" was usually preferred. The word "black" had a negative connotation among African Americans until the 1960s when the modern Civil Rights movement led some whites to become more accepting of black culture. There were faint signs of this as early as 1939 when the black singer, Marian Anderson, sang before a mixed audience of 75,000 in front of the Lincoln Memorial on Easter Sunday. She had been denied the privilege of singing in Constitution Hall in Washington D.C. which was owned by the Daughters of the American Revolution. Eleanor Roosevelt resigned her membership in that organization in protest. Within a short time, Marian Anderson was invited to sing in the White House before the King and Queen of England and was invited back. Recently there has been controversy over whether to capitalize "black" or "blacks." Because "white" or "whites" are rarely capitalized I have chosen not to capitalize "black" or "blacks." The most recent term is "African American." Because "black" is a shorter word, I have used it about half the time because it is more efficient. "African American" is longer but more precise. It refers to Americans whose ethnic, cultural and linguistic origins began in sub-Saharan Africa, much like Italian-Americans whose ethnic, cultural and linguistic origins began in Italy.

This is not to say there are no differences between African Americans and Italian Americans. Their histories and other characteristics, such as skin color and very often accents, are different. If any of these words are offensive to anyone, I apologize.

3. Leatha Crenshaw Hale, Interview by author concerning Maudine Brent, March 8, 2013

4. Powell, Betty F. *History of Mississippi County*. BNL Library Service, P.O. Box 1506, HARRY TRUMAN STATION, INDEPENDENCE, MISSOURI 64055, page 99

5. Patricia Montjoy, Interview by author, May 20, 2005

6. Shirley Cossey James, Interviews by author, March 26, 2004 & April 13, 2004

7. Leatha Crenshaw Hale, Interviews by author, November 7, 2005, & February 1, 2010

8. Mable Bradford Robinson, Interviews by author, March 18, 2014; April 21, 2014; August 2014, and a letter to author, July 1, 2014.

9. Adam Holman, Interview by author, March 18, 2014

10. Stepenoff, Bonnie. *Thad Snow: A Life of Social Reform.* University of Missouri Press, 2003, pp. 80, 83, 91-98, 135, 157-159. This book provides a thorough account of the 1939 Sharecropper's Strike (or Sharecropper's Demonstration.) To protest having been evicted from their homes in the middle of winter, both black and white sharecroppers lined highways 60 and 61 from Sikeston in Scott County to Hayti in Pemiscot County, a distance of 55 miles. The strikers and their families lived in makeshift shelters they had built along the highways. After five days, officials began removing the protesters using trucks provided by the State Highway Department and after two days had

removed 1,300 of them. Many were unable to return to their former homes because their landlords refused to take them back, so they went to various temporary encampments.

11. Adam Holman, Interview by author, March 18, 2014

12 Jerome Price, Interviews by author, May 6, 2014; June 7, 2014; September 25, 2014; and October 18, 2014

13 Leatha Crenshaw Hale, Interviews by author, February 1, 2010; March 8, 2010

14. Preston Heard Sr., Interviews by author, April 29, 2020; and May 6, 2020

15. Jerry and Maxine McDowell, Interviews by author; April 27, 2020; and May 6, 2020

# Part Two: 1957

## 4
## Murder

On Saturday evening, January 5, 1957, Johnny Malugen had a 9:30 date with June Castleberry, a senior at Sikeston High School. He drove from Charleston to Sikeston where he picked her up after her shift as a cashier at the Rex Movie Theater. They went for soft drinks at a small restaurant at the "South Y," where two roads joined and continued south. After finishing their drinks, they headed to Salcedo Road, turned left, and crossed the Frisco Railroad tracks. Johnny turned left again down a lover's lane on the northwest edge of town between the railroad tracks and a harvested cotton field. It was a dark, damp, chilly night. Johnny stopped, shut off the engine, and turned on the radio. June kicked off her shoes, took off her coat, and tucked her feet under her.

They had been parked little more than ten minutes when, at about 10:15, a dark figure approached the car, jerked open Johnny's door, and said *"Get out of the car, both of you. Now!"* Johnny shot back, *"No, you get out of here, Git!"* Johnny pulled the door shut, but the intruder jerked it open again. Giving June a quick glance, Johnny said, *"Give me the knife in the glove box."* But it was too late. The man backed up a few steps, raised his right arm, and fired a .32 caliber revolver pistol into Johnny's heart. June said, *"Are you hurt bad?"* Johnny answered, *"I don't know."* He started the car, drove about thirty feet, and collapsed over the steering wheel. The engine stalled.

June tried to start the car but couldn't. She would have opened the door and run, both to escape the scene and to seek help for Johnny, but she never had the chance. Her door was yanked open, and she was forcefully pulled out into the cold night. A man began dragging her across the cotton field, and after about 75 yards threw her down and tried to rape her, but she kicked him off. He got up, grabbed her around the neck, and continued dragging her across the field toward a shack on the edge of Sikeston's "Sunset Addition,[1]" or "Colored Town." There he threw her down on the porch and hit her in the face. June was too exhausted to resist, and the man raped her on the hard wooden floor of the porch. His deed done, he said, "If you tell anyone, I'll kill you." Just before he fled, he said, "I gotta a long way to go and I gotta get there fast; I'm going to St. Louis."[2]

As soon as the terrified girl got her bearings, she began running, across the cotton stubble and down the farm road beside the railroad tracks. June had run somewhere between a quarter and a half-mile[3] by the time she reached North Street on the northwest side of town. There she saw the tractor part of a truck waiting for a freight train to pass. June immediately began waving her arms and screaming. Mr. and Mrs. Henry Cooper, the occupants of the truck tractor, saw the panic on the breathless girl's face. She wore neither coat nor shoes, her nylons were shredded, and her clothes were covered with mud. Mr. Cooper rolled down his window and asked, "Can we help you?" June answered, in a loud, frightened voice, "Some Negro shot my boyfriend and attacked me!" Mr. Cooper said, "Get in. We'll go to the police.[4]"

En route to the police station, the Coopers met a squad car going the opposite direction. It was driven by Assistant Police Chief Alvin Mills. With him were officer Bill Kiefer and a state liquor inspector, Albert Cottle. When Mr. Cooper told the officers what June had told him, Officer Mills briefly interviewed June who told him where the crime had been committed. Mills told Mr. Cooper to join the officers in the squad car and accompany them to the crime scene. He asked Mrs. Cooper to take June to the hospital. After being treated at the hospital, June was declared to be as good as could be expected. By that time it was about 10:45. [5] Mr. Cooper, the officers, and Mr. Cottle found the spot June had described on the well-known lover's lane. Johnny's car sat there with both front doors open. Johnny's lifeless body was hanging out of the car, his right arm still hooked around the steering wheel. Officer Mills radioed Sikeston Police Headquarters to alert them to the situation and asked them to call Clyde Poe, the Scott County coroner.[6]

Sikeston Police Chief Arthur Bruce[7] soon joined the others at the scene. A sweep of the area with flashlights revealed smashed cotton stalks in the field beside the road and a path of broken stalks leading toward the Sunset Addition. About halfway through the field, they saw a place where the cotton stalks were more beaten down and the path widened. It looked as though the girl's attacker had struggled with her there before dragging her the rest of the way to a shack where two overturned chairs on the porch suggested a scuffle.

As would be expected, newspaper accounts of the murder and rape, did not correspond exactly: The *St. Louis Post-Dispatch* reported that "the assailant ordered her to turn off the lights and get out of the machine. 'I'll kill you just like I did your boyfriend,' he threatened. Nearly hysterical, the girl had difficulty finding the light switch [but] finally turned off the lights. The man then pulled her from the machine into the cotton stubble and attempted to attack her." No other account mentions turning off the lights. Unfortunately, the author no longer possesses that issue of the *St. Louis Post-Dispatch.* Mr. Poe arrived shortly, and with the police officers, Mr. Cooper, and Mr. Cottle looking on, the coroner assessed the situation, and radioed for the medical examiner, Dr. A. B. Smith, to join them. Within the hour, Dr. Smith came, pronounced Johnny dead, and had his body transported by a specialized ambulance resembling a hearse to the Nunnelee Funeral Home in Sikeston.

Early Sunday morning, January 6, Mr. Poe called a coroner's jury to view the body at the Delta Community Hospital. Dr. Smith performed a partial autopsy and found a .32 caliber lead bullet lodged in the base of Johnny's heart. The bullet had entered his left side, passed through his arm, and caused one lung to collapse before penetrating his heart. The autopsy results indicated that the hemorrhaging was so severe that Johnny probably bled to death within ten minutes.

Mr. Poe had not yet scheduled a date for the inquest but said it would probably be held the following week.[8]

## Endnotes

1. At the time, this part of town was also known as "Razor Town," referring to the stereotype of black men as carrying a razor in their boots. Frank Nickell, interview by author, July 8, 2010.

2. These details came from June Castleberry's account as reported in *The Daily Sikeston Standard,* January 7, 1957; *Enterprise-Courier,* January 10, 1957.

3. This estimate of the distance June ran was made by the author from an inspection of a 1955 map of Sikeston drawn by Howard Grant and kindly given to the author by George Weber Gilmore Jr. in 2014.

4. *The Daily Sikeston Standard,* January 7, 1957; *Enterprise-Courier,* January 10, 1957.

5. *The Daily Sikeston Standard,* January 7, 1957.

6. *The Daily Sikeston Standard,* January 7, 1957; *Enterprise-Courier,* January 10, 1957; T*he Missourian,* January 8, 1957.

7. Arthur Bruce (1918-2010) was Sikeston Chief of Police from 1956 to 1973. He served on Governor Warren Hearnes' Crime Commission along with Senator John Danforth and was Harry Truman's personal bodyguard when he visited Southeast Missouri. Bruce served in the Army during peacetime from 1934 to 1937, but when World War II broke out, he reenlisted and served from 1942 until 1946 to fight in the South Pacific. Later in life he received a bronze plaque for his involvement and dedication to thousands of children in Little League programs. He coached and managed teams of all ages and was vice president of the Girls Softball League. Bruce was elected to

the SEMO Amateur Baseball Hall of Fame in 1984. He was a member of the First Baptist Church of Bertrand, Missouri. [*Southeast Missourian* 6/10/10] .

8. T*he Daily Sikeston Standard,* January 7, 1957; *Enterprise-Courier*, January 10, 1957].

# 5

# Manhunt Begins

Immediately after finding Johnny's body, Sikeston Police Chief Arthur Bruce activated his entire police force and summoned help from police stations in nearby communities while Scott County Sheriff John Dennis[1] called all sheriff's offices in the area and available State Highway Patrolmen from Troop E headquartered in Poplar Bluff.

Sheriff John Dennis and his Deputy Aubrey Michael, Sheriff Ernest Scott of Mississippi County, accompanied by Deputy Ervin Smith, and Paul Long of the Charleston Police, and Sheriff Jim McDaniel of Stoddard County with deputies Ralph Temple and Ben Vaughn, and Chief of Police O. E. Stinnett of Morehouse arrived during the night.

At about the same time the crime was committed, a southbound Frisco freight train had made its pass through Sikeston. Its next stop was Hayti/Caruthersville, and thinking the assailant may have hopped the train, Bruce ordered it thoroughly searched when it stopped at the station there. June's early description had been brief and sketchy, but officials were told to search the train for a Negro male about six feet tall. He would likely have scratches about his face and neck.

Chief Bruce ordered his officers to check all buses scheduled to leave Sikeston for unidentified passengers and Scott County Sheriff John Dennis organized a search party comprised of officials from surrounding towns. By midnight what was to become the most exhaustive manhunt in the recent history of the area had begun, and by Sunday morning almost 100 law enforcement officers had arrived in Sikeston.

Sheriff Dennis ordered his men to block all roads into and out of Sikeston and to stop and question anyone trying to enter or leave town. Roadblocks in Charleston and other southeast Missouri towns were erected, and check points were set up on bridges and roads crossing state lines into Illinois, Kentucky, Tennessee, and Arkansas.

Word of the murder had reached Charleston before midnight. Early Sunday morning, at one of the roadblocks, authorities turned back several carloads of angry men and students from Charleston who were wrought up and yelling that they were "going to do something."[2]

By Sunday morning, word of Johnny's murder had reached the small town of Wyatt. A Charleston High School student, Shirley Cossey, said, "The first thing I remember was at the Baptist Church in Wyatt the day after the murder. Several people were riled up and were riling other people up. They said there would be trouble the next morning when school started, and I got the feeling they might be the ones to start it. They were so riled up that my father was afraid for me to go to school the next day, but I went anyway."[3]

* * *

At daybreak, the Sunset Addition, where most African Americans in Sikeston lived, was completely sealed off.

Sunday evening about eight o'clock, a resident of Sikeston's Sunset Addition reported to the Highway Patrol that he had just seen a black man hiding under the cotton compress warehouse on Felker Street near the vicinity of the crime. The man was found and arrested by Sheriff Dennis, Police Chief Bruce, and Lt. E. H. Damph of the State Highway Patrol. When questioned, the man said he was "scared and didn't know what to do," so he hid. According to the Sikeston and Charleston newspapers, the man was identified as Claude "Bootmouth" (or "Big Mouth") Lightsey and was taken to Jefferson City for two hours of questioning with the aid of a polygraph or lie detector machine. This approach yielded no information connecting him to the crime. Nevertheless, after Lightsey was brought back to Sikeston, June Castleberry was given an opportunity to see him and listen to him speak, but she was unable to identify him as her attacker.

Although exonerated of the crime, Claude was taken into Magistrate Court the following Tuesday to appear before Judge Marshall Montgomery.[4] where he pled guilty to a charge of gambling and was sentenced to a jail term.

A second black suspect, identified as "Highpockets," was picked up on Monday and questioned about a .32 caliber pistol he had in his possession but was later cleared of suspicion. This suspect, 58 years old and a friend of "Bootmouth," was not identified by any other name except "Highpockets" in either the *The Daily Sikeston Standard* or the *Enterprise-Courier.* He was taken into Magistrate

Court on Tuesday and charged with selling liquor without a license. His case was "held over."[5]

In running down all possible leads, the Highway Patrol was looking for a 1939 Chevrolet which was parked on the farm road the night of the murder and rape. A black couple in a pickup truck reported having seen a '39 Chevrolet leaving the vicinity of the crime about the time of the murder-rape. The couple had driven onto the farm road from the south, passed the Chevrolet, and then come upon a '49 Mercury with one door hanging open. They didn't report seeing Johnny's body, but the fact that the car door was hanging open and that they saw no one in the vicinity suggested that they had come upon Johnny's car after the murder but before the police arrived. The couple in the truck tried to go around Malugen's car but were afraid of getting stuck in the soft ground bordering the road. They backed up, and pulled up, and pulled across the railroad tracks. They told authorities that when they backed up, the 1939 Chevrolet they had passed, pulled out of the road and left. For obvious reasons, authorities were looking for the occupants of the car, hoping that they could give some lead to the murder-rape.[6]

"By this time authorities felt like they were looking for a needle in a haystack. They gave June a lie detector test to separate fact from emotion and hysteria but it failed to reveal any differences from her original statement to authorities."[7]

Events occurred so rapidly during the murder and rape that it was impossible for June or would have been for any woman in the midst of a murder and being dragged across a field of cotton stubble and raped, to keep track of events in a detailed way and in the right order.

Not surprisingly, an account in the *Saint Louis Post Dispatch* a day after the narrative in the *Daily Sikeston Standard* was accurate in a broad sense but differed in details.[8]

## Endnotes

1. John Clint Dennis (1917-2000) was the Scott County Missouri Sheriff from 1951 to 1976 during which he played a key role in the search and arrest of Lynn Wayne Hester and Joe Lester Slayton. In 1963 he was elected president of the Missouri Sheriff's Association. Dennis was a Marine during World War II and later served as a Missouri State Senator from 1976 to 1992. Dennis was appointed by Missouri Governor, James T. Blair, to the newly established Commission on Civil Rights. After his retirement he was elected to the Missouri State Senate. He died in Cape Girardeau, Missouri in 2000. [*Southeast Missourian,* 2000]

2. *The Daily Sikeston Standard,* January 7, 1957

3. Shirley Cossey James, Interviews by author, March 26, 2004 and April 13, 2004

4. Marshall Elmer "M.E." Montgomery (1888-1976) was Scott County Prosecuting Attorney and Superintendent of Schools before becoming a Magistrate Judge, a position he held for many years. During his career he had been a school teacher in Morley (where he was born), Claypool, and DeSoto. He was a veteran of World War I, a member the American Legion, a 32nd degree Mason, a member of the Scottish

Rite, and the First United Methodist Church of Sikeston. [*Southeast Missourian* 11/29/76]

5. *The Daily Sikeston Standard,* January 7, 1957; *Enterprise-Courier* January 10, 1957

6. *Enterprise-Courier January 10, 1957*

7. *Ibid.*

8. *St. Louis Post-Dispatch,* January 8, 1957

# 6
# Monday Morning

When I arrived at school a few minutes before nine o'clock on Monday morning, I was confronted with chaos. Students were congregated in front of the school and had been joined by some 60 or 70 students from Sikeston. When the black students arrived in a bus that had been provided for their safety, there were catcalls and jeers from the crowd.[1] Some of the boys from Wyatt made threats of physical violence against the black students. When the confrontation began, Coach Dee Bonner herded his athletes into the locker room. Some of the white basketball players declared they would quit the team rather than play with blacks.[2]

Superintendent of Schools John Harris Marshall, Principal Harding C. Williams, Coach Dee Bonner, and Assistant Coach James Humphrey had arrived at the school before the students did.[3] A large number of law enforcement officers were there as well. Mr. Marshall stood on one of the pedestals beside the front steps using a bullhorn to urge the students to calm down and go to class.[4] Mr. Marshall told us we would have to make up our work if we skipped class.[5]

Years after these events occurred, Glenn Ault told me, "Bud Story and I were on our way into the school through the side entrance when Mr. George Roberts, the Ag teacher, met us and told us to go to the Ag Building and stay there until he got back. We did. From my vantage point I saw a white student hit a black student who was on his way to the front entrance."[6] As would be expected, not all the students witnessed or remembered events the same way, especially 50 years later. One black student, Leatha Crenshaw, said she was quite certain there had been no physical violence, and if there had been, she would have known about it.[7] Glenn Ault added, "From the Ag building, I counted 24 blue State Highway Patrol cars, and they stayed there all day. And that's not counting the cars from the Charleston police and the sheriff's office."[8] John Goodin concurred, "I'd never seen so many State Patrol and police cars in one place in my life.[9]

There were similar disturbances at Sikeston High School that morning. According to school officials, 60 or 70 of the 675 students refused to enter the building when the bell rang. At that time Sikeston High School had 16 or 17 black students. When the other students walked through the crowd to enter the building, there were boos and catcalls. Some of the protesters yelled, "What do you want to go to nigger[1] and for?" Neither the principal Harold Kiehne, Coach Bill Sapp, or the teachers were successful in persuading every protesting student to come to class, but most of them did come inside. Some students returned home and others continued to protest outside.

Most of the Sikeston students, however, were quiet and respectful when Superintendent Lynn Twitty instructed them to abandon their boycott and return to class. He told them, "This is a democratic country in which all are entitled to an education. It is the law that we accept pupils of all races, and we endeavor to operate within the framework of the law." He told them that no law could compel them to go into the building that day, but if they did not, they would have to make up the class work they would miss.

Just as things were cooling down, several carloads of Charleston students drove into Sikeston and parked across from the school, but the city police told them to keep moving. They drove off, yelling and jeering, after which several carloads of Sikeston students headed for Charleston to join the protesters there. Officers stopped the cars at the Charleston city limits and told the students to return to Sikeston. When officers found two Sikeston boys with no ride, they took them to the edge of town and told them to hitchhike back to Sikeston.[10]

In Charleston, emotions ran high all day Monday. When Superintendent Marshall and Principal Williams escorted the black students through the crowd and into the school, the insults increased in volume. In spite of the frightening and hostile atmosphere, all the black students attended school that morning, but some of the white students insisted they would not return to shool until the six black students were sent elsewhere.11

According to Mr. Williams about 94 of Charleston's 350 students failed to enter the school after the final bell that morning. About an hour later, several more students left the school when their parents, concerned about the volatile situation, came to take them home.[12] One source reported that during the following days a few of the parents, both black and white, carried baseball bats in their cars when they took their children to and from school.[13] All but about 30 students returned to school for their afternoon classes.[14] Mr. Roberts recalled: "When the trouble started that morning, I told my Ag students to stay out of it. Then I went to the front entrance of the school and saw a small group of black students, a couple of girls and one or two boys, coming up the circular walkway toward the front door. A bunch of white boys, about 25 of 'em, were going down the walkway toward them, and there was also a bunch of white men across the street from the school egging them on. 'Keep those sonabitches out. Don't let 'em get in.' When I saw one of my students leading that pack of boys, I got hot. I went down there, grabbed him by the collar, and dragged him back into the high school. He was president of the FFA (Future Farmers of America) and one of my boys. I'd already told him to stay out of that mess. Then I went back to the Ag building and started my class. I told Bill Myers to go tell my students to get back in the school, but they wouldn't.".[15]

Most Charleston students did return to classes, but some of them joined the Sikeston students, formed a mob of about 150, and marched through the streets of Charleston for about an hour.[16] Some of the students were bent on intimidating black citizens and others just went along to vent their feelings or to see what would happen. On that morning, my mother was driving our black maid, Lilly B. Phillips, from her home to ours and suddenly found her car surrounded by unruly students. They began rocking the car, prompting my mother and Lilly B. to lock the doors. It was a frightening experience for my mother and even more so, I'm sure, for Lilly B.[17] My friend Paul Hill said:

"When we got back from rampaging, we all sat across from the high school on Main Street. Mr. Williams sent his secretary to bring me to his office. He told me to tell the kids to go home, come back to school tomorrow, and everything would be OK. I was the ringleader, and Mr. Williams had whipped me a few times. The students eventually came in, but not right away. We said a bunch of stupid, mean things like 'kill the 'N-words'[18] but it was all just bunch of damn talk. We was just so hurt, we didn't know what to do."[19]

Despite such unjust, chaotic, and nonproductive responses to the murder of a close friend, similar responses from others who have experienced such losses are not unusual, especially if the perpetrator and victim are of a different race.

Given how upset the Charleston students were after the murder, it should not be surprising to see how hurt and outraged the Sikeston students were. The horrendous crimes had, in fact, outraged both towns. The scope of the outrage in Sikeston can be seen in the magazine, *True Police Cases.* One of its articles, *Violent Skies Over Sikeston,* dated May 1957, reports the experience of one of its reporters, James J Abbott.[20]

"This was the scene I encountered on January 14, 1957, when I drove along U.S. Highway 60 into Sikeston, Missouri. On another occasion several years ago, I had visited this peaceful little city of 14,000, [three times as large as Charleston], situated in the southeastern part of Missouri. At that time, I had found the community courteous, cheerful and talkative. But now I immediately detected that, although the sun shone brightly and clear, there was a chill in the air not strictly due to the winter temperature. I could see that, in sharp contrast to my previous visit, the people seemed to have become taciturn, bordering on outright hostility. My best bet to get the facts was to try to thaw out the grimly sealed lips of the people who had been directly affected in one way or another by the terrible tragedy that settled on Sikeston. Slowly the residents with whom I spoke let down their guard; first they resented the presence of a stranger in their midst, but when they learned the purpose of my mission, the words tumbled torrent-like, spurred by a desire to unburden the load of venom which had seeped down the city's thoroughfare like a rattler on a rampage."

Charleston school officials reported that most of the close friends of Johnny Malugen, including members of the football team, returned to school without incident or protest. Most of the unruly students were only passing acquaintances of Johnny's.[21]

My friend, Bob Carlisle said, "I joined the march downtown, I guess because everybody else did, but a week or two later I looked back and thought it was stupid. I felt ashamed and guilty."[22] The majority of the students did not participate in the demonstrations and came to their classes when the protesters marched off. Reasons for their refusal to join the mob were varied. Some thought it was pointless or just plain wrong. Many students were told by their parents not to participate in any disturbance. John Goodin said, "My father told me to stay out of trouble."[23] Eleanor Switzer said, "I went right to Mr. Moss's English class. My parents would not have approved of my skipping class and doing that."[24] Fred Ferrell said, "I remember telling my friends - Bud Story, Glenn Ault, and Jim Cullison - that we are not going on any march because my parents would not approve, and we didn't.[25]" Bonnie Dernoncourt said, "My father told me in no uncertain terms, 'You will have nothing to do with any racial protests.' My main emotional reaction was fear because there was a murderer and rapist on the loose. If there was someone, black or white, running around killing and raping, I wanted to stay out of danger."[26] Doris Maxwell said, "I don't remember whether I walked downtown with the protesters that morning or not. If I did, it would have been to see what was happening. I wasn't the type to be prejudiced against someone just because of their color, especially if they had nothing to do with the murder."[27]

Most of the protesters went to their classes later that morning. When the 1:00 o'clock bell rang after lunch, all but some 30 students had returned to class. All six black students attended morning classes, and five returned after lunch.

A few days after Monday's disturbances, the Sikeston students who had demonstrated and stayed out of school were put on probation for the remainder of the year. Superintendent Twitty said he would take no further action against the students at that time, but if they caused further trouble, they would suffer the consequences. "The school will not expel such students," he said, "They will expel themselves."[28]

The story of the crimes, manhunt, and unrest at the schools was carried in newspapers from New Orleans to Chicago and quite a distance east and west.[29] An account of the crimes and following conflicts appeared in the *New York Times* on January 10, 1957.[30]

## Endnotes

1. *Enterprise-Courier*, January 10, 1957

2. Jim Cullison, Interview by author, June 2009

3. John Goodin, Interview by author, June 14, 2009

4. Glenn Ault, Interview by author, August 16, 2009

5. *Enterprise-Courier*, January 10, 1957

6. Glenn Ault, Interview by author, August 16, 2009

7. Leatha Crenshaw Hale, Interview by author, February 1, 2010

8. Glenn Ault, Interview by author, August 16, 2009

9. John Goodin, Interview by author, June 14, 2009

10. *The Daily Sikeston Standard*, January 7, 1957

11. *Enterprise-Courier,* January 10, 1957

12. *Ibid.*

13. Deborah Betts Turner, Interview by author, August 22, 2005

14. *Enterprise-Courier,* January 10, 1957

15. George Roberts, Interviews by author, December 27, 2009 & November 9, 2010

16. *The Daily Sikeston Standard,* January 7, 1957; *Enterprise-Courier,* January 10, 1957

17. Margaret Joslyn, January 7, 1957

18. The author is fully aware that it is improper and wrong to use the "N- word" in normal conversation or in writing.

However, this is a direct quote and therefore part of the historical record. I didn't use the word myself; I simply recorded the event as it occurred. It is history. Given the strength of modern political correctness, however, as you can see above, I omitted it.

19. Paul Hill , Interview by author, August 18, 2005

20. James J. Abbott, author of *Violent Skies Over Sikeston,* May 1957

21. *The Daily Sikeston Standard,* January 7, 1957

22. Bob Carlisle, Interview by author, 2002

23. John Goodin, Interview by author, June 14, 2009

24. Eleanor Switzer, Interview by author, 2004

25. Fred Ferrell, Interview by author, June 2009

26. Bonnie Story, Interview by author, May 21, 2009

27. Doris Maxwell, Interview by author, 2004

28. Enterprise-Courier, January 10, 1957

29. Ann Lese Joslyn, written notes, June 1 1957

30. In late November 2019, the author called the *New York Times* and spoke with the person in charge of back issues. She was very patient and spent at least 20 minutes looking for the article and then gave me a way to look for the article myself. The person with whom I spoke said there were so many articles in the *Times* covering both national and international news that retrieving one of them, especially sixty-two years after the event would be very difficult. It is also possible that my sister, Ann Lese Joslyn, got the date wrong.

# 7

# Funeral

Johnny's coffin was open for viewing on Sunday night, the day after the murder, at the Nunnelee Funeral Home in Charleston, and the visitation was held the same evening.[1] Johnny's father had personally invited our black schoolmates to attend the visitation.[2] The body lay in state at the funeral home until the time of the funeral. The funeral was scheduled for Tuesday afternoon and the high school students were dismissed at 1:20 p.m. to attend the 2:00 p.m. service at the First Baptist Church. My sister and I sat on the front row but didn't see the students behind us. More than 750 people attended the funeral, many of whom had come from neighboring towns. The First Baptist Church was not large enough to accommodate the crowd, so the overflow went to the First Methodist Church across the street where a public address system had been set up. The Chaffee High School football coach attended the funeral and brought the co-captains of his team. The Rev. D. B. Bledsoe delivered the sermon and summarized his message with, "Life comes only from God. We shall not take that which we cannot give back to another."

Six members of the 1956 Charleston High School football team served as pallbearers: Wallace Brazel, Jimmy Chandler, Paul Hill, Paul Lee Moore, Bill Myers, and Al Francis Pannier. The remaining members of the football team formed a court of honor.

Marilyn Story, a classmate of Johnny's, sang "Nearer My God to Thee" and "I Walked Today Where Jesus Walked." The organist was Miss Olline Cain.[3] Paul Hill said:

> "We all went to the funeral. There was no loud crying or anything like that. We were just *sad, very sad.* We had lost a friend. Yeah, some of us had tears in our eyes, but we didn't cry out loud. After the funeral and after the burial at the cemetery there were a lot of hugs. Hugs between girls and hugs between a boy and a girl. The boy's gave 'shoulder hugs' between each other like where one boy would put his hand up on another boys shoulder and experience condolences, like 'Joe, we've lost a really good friend and we'll miss him.'"[4]

The author, myself, did not go to the cemetery: After the funeral, I went to my dad's law office on Main Street where we watched the funeral procession of over a hundred cars following the hearse to the International Order of Odd Fellows (IOOF) Cemetery, where Johnny's body was to be interred. As the cars went by, Dad said, "I'm sure this is a sad day for Johnny's parents."

Dad wasn't liberal on racial matters, but he was supportive of me during the trouble at the high school, and he didn't approve of the way the black students were being treated. In his business dealings he was fair. When anybody came into his office, he would defend him or her at trial or do other legal work they may have needed. It didn't matter whether they were black or white. At Dad's funeral in 1980, a lawyer friend of his, Jim Ed Reeves, gave the eulogy and said that within Dad's own framework of thinking he had an innate sense of justice.

By the time of the funeral, the senior class had collected more than a hundred dollars as a memorial. Schoolmates continued to collect money to buy a beautiful gravestone. On one corner is etched a pair of track shoes and on another a football. At the top is an etching of Johnny's senior class ring, and in the center, inlaid in the stone, is his senior portrait.[5] (See photograph after the Epilogue.)

* * *

Jane Cooper, now Stacy, had graduated from Charleston High School the year before Johnny was killed. Jane said: "Johnny and I were wonderful friends and he had dated my best friend, Harriet Goodin. We were all very close, and when Harriet's father died in 1954, we helped her sort it out."

There was a lot of prejudice in our school and a lot of resentment had built up against the blacks for 'pushing their way into our school.' Johnny's murder just capped it off. After the funeral, I got in a car with some of my friends, and we went to the Badlands[6] just waiting for anyone to walk out and do something. There was so much anger in that car! It was the only time in my life I could have just jumped out and grabbed someone. I've often thought that if I'd been a part of seriously hurting a black person, I could never have gotten it out of my mind. I learned from that experience that we all have prejudice that we are not aware of and that we shouldn't consider ourselves immune to it.[7]

* * *

The front page article on the Tuesday, January 8, 1957 issue of *The Daily Sikeston Standard* read:

"A peculiar feeling of uneasy quiet prevailed this morning over Sikeston and Charleston following the announcement that exhaustive tests of the first two suspects in the murder and rape case of Saturday night had apparently cleared them of any complicity in the crimes. While the surface may be calm, however, there is intensive activity going on in law enforcement circles as city police, sheriff's deputies, and State Highway Patrolmen track down and investigate every clue received, no matter how small. The danger point, if there is any, according to the officers, lies in the period following the funeral of the victim at Charleston this afternoon, and all officers, including special details of the State Patrol, have been alerted for possible trouble and to quell any demonstrations immediately.".[8]

Endnotes

1. John Goodin, Interview by author June 14, 2009

2. Erma Malugen Vaughn, Interview by author, April 3, 2010

3. *Enterprise-Courier,* January 10, 1957

4. Paul Hill, Interview by author, December 9, 2019

5. Lese Joslyn, written notes, June 1, 1957

6. "Badland" referred to the black or "colored" part of town and sometimes to an area in this part of town with night clubs and bars where there were often fights on Saturday nights. "Colored Town" was the polite way to refer to that part of town. "Black" was not in fashion at that time.

7. Jane Cooper Stacy, Interview by author, July 21, 2010

8. *The Daily Sikeston Standard,* January 8, 1957

# 7.5
# Photos 1957 or Before

Odell Wadkins 1979

1960s—Alice Faris, Hallie Hisey, Mable Roberts, Mattie Henry, Lella Harris

Five school teachers who taught the seventh and eighth grades at the Eugene Field School for many years. Miss Mattie Henry, fourth from left, is smiling!

Johnny Malugen 1956

June Castleberry 1956

URI, MONDAY, JANUARY 7, 1957 — *Sikeston Standard* — NUMBER 89

# DER-RAPE SUSPECT

JOHNNY MALUGEN, VICTIM OF NEGRO ASSASSIN

## Nearly 100 Law Officers In Manhunt for Slayer of Youth, Attacker of Girl

The vicious, senseless slaying of Johnny Malugen, 18-year old Charleston High School student, and the forcible criminal assault upon his 18-year old girl companion Saturday night by an, as yet, unidentified Negro, touched off the most extensive and determined manhunt by nearly 100 law officers that continued from midnight Saturday until after midnight Sunday and resulted in the apprehension of two Negro suspects.

First information of the crime came when Mr. and Mrs. Henry Cooper, of 221 N. Handy street, shortly before 11 p.m. while they were waiting at the North street crossing for a Frisco freight train to pass, picked up the girl who had been the Negro's victim.

They took her on to town where they met a police car driven by Assistant Chief Alvin Mills, who had with him Officer Bill Kiefer and Albert Cottle, state liquor inspector. The girl told Mills, "My boy friend has been shot."

Leaving the hysterical girl with Mrs. Cooper, the officers, with Mr. Cooper, raced to the scene of the reported crimes which was on the north and south dirt road paralelling the Frisco railroad back to the old warehouse at the north end of Frisco street.

They found that Johnny Malugen was dead and the coroner, Clyde Poe, was called. He had the body removed to Nunnelee Funeral Home where, Sunday morning, a coroner's jury, composed of Bill Vandevort, J. F. Cox Jr., Dick McDougal, Milam Limbaugh, Bill Hodges and Melburn Arbaugh viewed the body. The inquest, it is reported, will be held later this week.

It was discovered the bullet, later found to be from a 32 caliber pistol, went through the boy's left arm and on into his chest, causing an internal hemorrhage from which, it is believed, he bled to death in ten minutes after being shot.

The girl told the officers Trooper Copeland and Officers Bailey and Woodward of the city police that she and Malugen were seated in the parked car, listening to the radio. The windows were closed, she said, and the Negro came [illegible]

until she encountered the Coopers.

Immediately the word of the [illegible] crime came in, every city policeman was ordered on duty by Chief of Police Arthur Bruce and, in addition, a score of Auxiliary Policemen were placed on duty to block off all roads leading out of the city.

Help came promptly from the State Highway Patrol with all available officers of Troop E being ordered here to assist in apprehending the Negro.

Sheriff John Dennis and Deputy Aubrey Michael were on hand and Sheriff Ernest Scott, of Mississippi county, accompanied by Deputy Ervin Smith and Paul Long of the Charleston Police; Sheriff Jim McDaniel of Stoddard county, and deputies Ralph Temple and Ben Vaughn; Chief of Police O. E. Stinnett of Morehouse, and officers from East Prairie arrived during the night.

Every car or individual leaving the city by any of the highways was stopped and questioned and Negroes were turned back in to Sunset Addition.

Sunday morning at daylight, the officers blocked off the entire Sunset Addition and conducted a street by street, house to house search, but with this shake down completed, there was no arrest, although a number of persons were closely questioned

**FOUL PLAY POSSIBLE IN STANDARD COLLECTIONS**

**It has been reported, in several instances, that unauthorized boys are out collecting money from Standard subscribers. They represent neither the Standard nor the Sikeston News Service. Be sure you receive an adequate receipt for any payments made and try to identify the collector in the event he might be an imposter.**

## Sikeston Youth Signed Up as Ass't. Coach

James E. Lee, 24, of Sikeston, Mo., was hired as assistant coach and American history teacher for the high school at a special meeting of the Minonk Dana Rutland school board, following the basketball game, Friday night, according to The Minonk (Ill.) News Dispatch.

Lee will report for duty when school re-opens, Jan. 2, after the holidays. He fills the vacancy created by the departure of Asst. Coach John Galbraith, who was called up for military service

## Dr. Salk Has New Idea on

Front page *The Daily Sikeston Standard,* January 7, 1957

No. 300
10.48

FILED JAN 21 1957

THE DIVISION OF HEALTH OF MISSOURI
STANDARD CERTIFICATE OF DEATH

State File No. 3355

BIRTH NO. ____ REG. DIST. NO. 333 PRIMARY REG. DIST. NO. 3074 Registrar's No. 4

WRITE PLAINLY—USING UNFADING BLACK INK—MAKE A PERMANENT RECORD

1. PLACE OF DEATH
a. COUNTY Scott
b. CITY (If outside corporate limits, write RURAL and give township) OR TOWN Sikeston
c. LENGTH OF STAY (in this place) 2 Hrs.
d. FULL NAME OF (If not in hospital or institution, give street address or location) HOSPITAL OR INSTITUTION Field near Sikeston

2. USUAL RESIDENCE (Where deceased lived. If institution: residence before admission).
a. STATE Missouri
b. COUNTY Mississippi
c. CITY OR TOWN Charleston
d. Is Residence within limits of a city or incorporated town? Yes [X] No [ ]
e. STREET ADDRESS (If rural, give location) 301 E. Byrd Avenue

3. NAME OF DECEASED (Type or Print) a. (First) John b. (Middle) Robert c. (Last) Malugen
4. DATE OF DEATH (Month) (Day) (Year) Jan. 5, 1957
5. SEX Male
6. COLOR OR RACE White
7. MARRIED, NEVER MARRIED, WIDOWED, DIVORCED (Specify) Never Married
8. DATE OF BIRTH June 12, 1938
9. AGE (In years last birthday) 18 If under 1 year: Months 6 Days 23 If under 24 hrs.: Hours Min.
10a. USUAL OCCUPATION (Give kind of work done during most of working life, even if retired) Student
10b. KIND OF BUSINESS OR INDUSTRY — — — —
11. BIRTHPLACE (City and State or Foreign Country) Caruthersville, Missouri
12. CITIZEN OF WHAT COUNTRY? USA
13a. FATHER'S NAME Guffrie Malugen
13b. MOTHER'S MAIDEN NAME Gertrude McGee
14. NAME OF HUSBAND OR WIFE — — — — —
15. WAS DECEASED EVER IN U.S. ARMED FORCES? (Yes, no, or unknown) No (If yes, give war or dates of service) None
16. SOCIAL SECURITY NO. 489-40-1603
17. INFORMANT'S SIGNATURE OR NAME Raymond Vinson ADDRESS Charleston, Mo.

MEDICAL CERTIFICATION

18. CAUSE OF DEATH
Enter only one cause per line for (a), (b), and (c)
*This does not mean the mode of dying, such as heart failure, asthenia, etc. It means the disease, injury, or complication which caused death.

I. DISEASE OR CONDITION DIRECTLY LEADING TO DEATH* (a) Bullet from 32 caliber pistol passed through left upper arm, left lung and heart. Found in pericardial sac.
ANTECEDENT CAUSES
Morbid conditions, if any, giving rise to the above cause (a) stating the underlying cause last.
DUE TO (b)
DUE TO (c)
II. OTHER SIGNIFICANT CONDITIONS
Conditions contributing to the death but not related to the disease or condition causing death.
INTERVAL BETWEEN ONSET AND DEATH 0

19a. DATE OF OPERATION
19b. MAJOR FINDINGS OF OPERATION 981X
20. AUTOPSY? Yes [X] No [ ]

21a. ACCIDENT SUICIDE HOMICIDE (Specify) Homicide
21b. PLACE OF INJURY (e.g., in or about home, farm, factory, street, office bldg., etc.) Field
21c. (CITY, TOWN, OR TOWNSHIP) Sikeston (COUNTY) Scott (STATE) Mo
21d. TIME OF INJURY (Month) (Day) (Year) (Hour) Jan. 5, 1957 -
21e. INJURY OCCURRED WHILE AT WORK [ ] NOT WHILE AT WORK [X]
21f. HOW DID INJURY OCCUR? Shot by assailant while sitting in car

22. I hereby certify that I attended the deceased from ____, 19__, to ____, 19__, that I last saw the deceased alive on ____, 19__, and that death occurred at 10:00 Pm., from the causes and on the date stated above.

23a. SIGNATURE (Degree or title) Thelma C. Rueckthorpe, M.D. Health Officer
23b. ADDRESS Benton, Mo
23c. DATE SIGNED 1-9-57

24a. BURIAL, CREMATION, REMOVAL (Specify) Burial
24b. DATE 1-8-57
24c. NAME OF CEMETERY OR CREMATORY I O O F Cemetery
24d. LOCATION (City, town, or county) (State) Charleston, Missouri

DATE REC'D BY LOCAL REG. 1-10-57
REGISTRAR'S SIGNATURE Mrs. Ella Hunter
25. FUNERAL DIRECTOR'S SIGNATURE Edward E. Hunnicutt ADDRESS Nunnelee Funeral Chapel Charleston, Mo.
(Licensed Embalmer's Statement on Reverse Side)

Johnny's Death Certificate 1957

Johnny's Tombstone 1957

# 8
# Crying Wolf

Law enforcement officials were correct in their belief that there could be trouble after Johnny's funeral.

In Wyatt, just as it began to get dark, a thirteen-year-old white girl and her eleven-year-old sister were riding their bicycles. The younger girl started screaming and adults began to emerge from their houses. The girls loudly asserted that a black man had come out of the darkness, grabbed the older sister, torn her clothes, and made crude remarks. Her dress was torn on the left side, but she was otherwise unharmed. The attack reportedly occurred in front of the blacksmith shop near the Raffety cotton gin.

Law enforcement was called immediately. Mississippi County Sheriff Scott, his deputies, Charleston police officers, and the State Highway Patrol converged on Wyatt and began a vigorous search for the assailant. As soon as the authorities arrived, carloads of angry men began pouring into Wyatt and quickly filled up what little parking space there was around the gin. They got out of their cars and stood around in small groups, their silence exuding a sense of foreboding as a light rain fell in the darkness. Finally, about eleven o'clock, it began raining hard, which prompted the men to get back in their cars and go home. No suspects were found, but the officers said they would come back in the morning.[1, 2] *On Thursday, the police and the sheriff's office questioned the two Wyatt girls more thoroughly than they had been able to do the night before. Mississippi County Sheriff Ernest Scott[5] said the 13-year-old girl and her 11-year-old sister, both in the fourth grade, could not keep their stories straight. Their accounts did not stay consistent from one telling to another or between the two girls. Among other things, the investigators could not figure out how the older girl's dress could have been torn by an assailant since it was covered by a coat. It appeared that the dress was torn, not from an assault but by becoming entangled in the rear wheel of the bicycle.[3]

The *Chaffee Signal* referred the alleged assault as fact, stating that "a Negro man came out of the darkness, grabbed the older girl, tore off her blouse, and made indecent remarks." There was no follow-up to the story.[4] Although Sheriff Ernest Scott[5] had serious reservations about the validity of the girls' account, he did offer a $500 reward to anyone furnishing information leading to the arrest and conviction of the man who had assaulted the girls, if in fact there was such an assailant. He speculated, however, that either the story was a hoax or the girls were so excited and frightened that their imaginations got the better of them. Later that Wednesday, the younger girl admitted that there had been no assault at all.[6]

* * *

After hearing rumors of possible additional disturbances, Charleston High School Principal Williams requested that police and State Patrolmen be available when school started Wednesday morning. Five patrol cars under the direction of Lt. E. F. Damph and Sgt. Gene Harris, arrived well ahead of the students. Instead of staying in their cars, as they had Monday, they got out on the school grounds, prepared for action. Four of the black students - Louis Craft, Patricia Montjoy, Mable Bradford, and Leatha Crenshaw - came to school as a group and were confronted by a crowd of white boys. The boys shoved and pushed Louis then told all of them to go home. At this point, Mr. Williams, with the assistance of some white senior boys, persuaded the roughnecks to allow the black students to pass through the crowd. When Katie Davis got off the school bus, a group of white girls stood on the front steps and blocked her entrance to the school. During the standoff, some of the other students shouted, "Don't let her in; don't let her in." Finally, several teachers broke up the blockade and Katie went in. Mr. Williams said he felt sure that the trouble Wednesday morning resulted from the anger stirred up by the incident in Wyatt the night before. He said he didn't think there would be any more trouble but that police protection should continue.[7]

## Endnotes

1.*The Daily Sikeston Standard,* January 9, 1957; *Enterprise-Courier,* January 10, 1957

2. The January 9th account of the alleged assault ended with, "No suspects were found, but the officers said they would come back in the morning." In later reports, however, there was no mention of whether the officers came back.

3. *The Daily Sikeston Standard,* January 9, 1957; *Enterprise-Courier.* January 10, 1957

4. *Chaffee Signal, January 17, 1957*

5. James Ernest Scott (1893-1973) had been mayor of East Prairie, Missouri before he was elected Sheriff of Mississippi County in 1940. He served in that capacity until 1959 when he retired. He was a well-known landowner in the area and a member of the church of God. [*Southeast Missourian* 11/12/73]

6. *The Daily Sikeston Standard,* January 11, 1957; *Enterprise-Courier,* January 10, 1957

7. *Ibid*

# 9

# Only One Is Guilty

The senselessness of the protests and intimidation of black students was duly noted by Charleston's *Enterprise-Courier*. On January 10, it quoted one of the officers involved in the case: "Charleston High School students are doing more to hamper and impede the search for the party who killed John Malugen than any other single factor." The paper noted that "For this past week four to seven patrol cars, from ten to twenty patrolmen, at least one police car, and one or two local officers have been stationed at the high school as a preventative measure. Inciting additional trouble, however trivial, will accomplish only one thing: it will continue to tie up valuable manpower desperately needed elsewhere."

The same issue of the *Enterprise-Courier* included the following editorial:

**Only One Is Guilty**

Both Sikeston and Charleston have been sitting on powder kegs since last Saturday night after the senseless murder of friendly, likable John Malugen, and the rape of his girlfriend by a perverted sex maniac.

This is the time for somber, serious reflection.

This is no time to incite additional trouble. Mob action will only serve to compound an already vicious situation.

All of us, in school and out, liked Johnny Malugen. Of that there is no doubt. He was a fine, clean young man who had intended to devote his life to coaching—dealing with the next generation of young men and women. That was not in the cards to him, and it is only natural that we seek an outlet for this emotional strain and upset.

But additional murder, arson, and violence will settle absolutely nothing. It will not settle the problem of integrated schools. It can only bring shame and disgrace and suffering and terror to many innocent persons.

Thus far this situation has been handled as it should have been handled, in an orderly fashion and according to the law. To be highly commended are members of the Missouri State Highway Patrol and the hundred or so additional police officers of the area. It must be mentioned also that Negro leaders, ministers, teachers, and businessmen in Sikeston and Charleston have cooperated fully. They are as concerned as all of the rest are concerned, that the party guilty of this heinous crime be found, identified, tried by due process of law—and speedily executed.

No self-respecting Negro in either community likes to be associated, even named in the same breath, with the human scum who perpetrated the initial crimes. They would go to any length to find him, and to be instrumental in turning him over to the authorities.

The first big emotional shock wave is past.

The real test of leadership is yet to come. May God grant that no emotional stress or strain get out of hand, and in doing so, touch off something all of us will live to regret.

Keep this one fact in mind: only ONE person is guilty of the crime of murder and rape.

Let that person be found and punished.

And only that one.[1]

Endnote

1. *Enterprise-Courier,* January 10, 1957

# 10
# The Last Good Lead

On Tuesday, January 8th Sikeston Mayor Charles Butler encouraged "all citizens white and colored," to assist in finding the "sex fiend" who had murdered Johnny Malugen and raped June Castleberry. He urged any residents who had information that might possibly shed light on the investigation to report it to Sheriff John Dennis, Chief of Police Arthur Bruce, the State Highway Patrol, or to himself. The mayor said he felt sure that some of the black citizens of the area knew something that could assist in the manhunt. He promised confidentiality and protection to any black resident who might come forth with information.[1]

On Wednesday, Colonel Hugh Waggoner, Chief of the Missouri State Highway Patrol, visited Charleston and Sikeston to assess the situation. Upon returning to Jefferson City, he issued a statement congratulating all the law enforcement agencies for their high level of cooperation in the manhunt. He cautioned that the State Patrol had other ongoing duties and that any more demonstrations or disturbances would take officers away from the search for the murderer-rapist.[2]

By Thursday, law enforcement officials had questioned a large number of suspects. Although two were still in custody, neither appeared to be guilty, and officials said it seemed as though they were looking for a "needle in a haystack." They continued to sift evidence no matter how trivial it seemed. Anyone suspected of concealing information relating to the crime was made to submit to a lie detector test. None of those tested were proven to be hiding anything.

On Thursday, the search for the murderer and rapist regained momentum when a suspect was apprehended in St. Louis. He was a black employee of a small arms plant there. The plant was closed on weekends, but the suspect failed to come to work on the Monday and Tuesday following the murder. He came to work on Wednesday and applied at the plant clinic for treatment of deep and multiple scratches on his neck. The plant's chief of security, knowing about the manhunt in southeast Missouri and the description of the suspect, called the St. Louis Police Department.

The man was apprehended and by Friday morning had been thoroughly questioned. Investigators were not satisfied with his story about how, when, and where he was scratched. The suspect said he was scratched when a man strong-armed and knocked him down on a sidewalk. Because June had reported that she had scratched her attacker around the neck, the police held the suspect and continued their investigation.[3]

On Friday, Sheriff John Dennis and State Trooper M. W. Copeland drove June and her mother to the homicide bureau of the St. Louis Police Department. Chief of Detectives James Chapman and Sergeant William Moran presented June with a lineup which included the suspect, hoping that she could identify him as the wanted man, but she was unable to do so. She described her attacker as lighter in build and color than any of the men in the lineup.[4]

## Endnotes

1. *The Daily Sikeston Standard,* January 8, 1957

2. *The Daily Sikeston Standard, January 10, 1957; The Daily Sikeston Standard, January 12, 1957, Enterprise-Courier, January 10, 1957*

3. *The Daily Sikeston Standard, January 11, 1957; Chaffee Signal,* January 24, 1957

4. *Ibid.*

# 11
# A Peaceful Monday

In contrast to the chaos at Charleston High School on the Monday after the murder, the next Monday, a week later, was peaceful. Many of my schoolmates crowded together in the front hallway but went promptly to their classes when the bell rang. There had been rumors during the weekend that there would be more trouble that morning, but when the six black students arrived, all in one car, they had no difficulty entering the school.

That morning twelve State Highway Patrol cars, two police cars, and sheriff's deputies were on hand. Their presence may have had some bearing on the students' orderly behavior, but there were no overt indications that a protest or demonstration had been planned.[1]

For the rest of that spring semester, before and after school and during the noon hour, a number of law enforcement officers continued to keep an eye on places where students walked or congregated. They hoped their presence would help prevent any racial incidents from escalating.

Endnote

1. *The Daily Sikeston Standard,* January 14, 1957

# 12
# Five Final Suspects

During the ten days immediately following Johnny's murder, the manhunt was intense and far-reaching. On Tuesday, January 15, two suspects from Mississippi County were picked up and brought in for questioning. One was let go, and the other was released after having passed a lie detector test concerning his whereabouts on the night of the crime. On Thursday, three more suspects were questioned and subjected to polygraph tests, but none appeared to be tied to the crime. Two of the men were released, but the third was tried in Magistrate Court in Charleston, convicted on an adultery charge, and sentenced to 30 days in jail.

Law enforcement officials continued to urge citizens to share any information they had, even if they didn't think it was important. Those involved in the manhunt continued their tedious and painstaking search for clues and followed up on every lead. Officers across a wide area, and in all directions, remained on the lookout for a black man fitting June's description of the murderer. The search continued as far as the Arkansas state line and in many Missouri counties north and west.

Despite the dogged work of many state troopers, police, and sheriff's deputies, leads dwindled and came to a halt as the days, weeks, and months, passed. Media coverage became less frequent, but investigators continued their work on the case, determined to find, apprehend, and bring to trial the Negro guilty of the murder of Johnny Malugen and the rape of June Castleberry.[1]

## Endnote

1. T*he Daily Sikeston Standard,* January 16, 1957

# 13
# A Long Spring

With a constant undercurrent of discontent, the atmosphere that spring semester at Charleston High School was stressful for black and white students alike. There was a continual low-grade harassment of the black students, which kept them painfully aware that they were not welcome.

Those times were not only stressful for the students but also for the teachers and administrators. Years later, I asked Mr. Warren Moss, our English and speech teacher from Mississippi, what he remembered about those days. He said he had to patrol the hallways in case there was an altercation between the black and white students.

Mr. Moss asked, "It was some blacks from Cairo that murdered Johnny, wasn't it?" I found that some people in Charleston thought that was true. I don't know where the idea came from, but my guess is that it was because racial problems in Cairo were much worse than in Charleston.

After the lunch hour, there were usually several students sitting on the front steps of the school waiting for the bell to ring. Sometimes, when the black students came up the steps, they were greeted with catcalls. Pat Montjoy told me that I had said, "Why don't you leave them alone?" I have no recollection of having said that but would be proud if I had.

Pat Montjoy told me: "The murder of Johnny Malugen opened up a whole new world to me, not a pretty one, one I had not experienced before. It was a shock to find that my white classmates, who had been friendly to me before the murder, turned on me and treated me like dirt. All of a sudden, I was an outcast. I couldn't believe it was happening. I didn't realize how strong the color line was."

One of Pat's white classmates had been having difficulty with plane geometry, a subject in which Pat excelled. The girl asked Pat for help. Pat helped her and felt her assistance was appreciated. Pat recalled, however, that "On the Friday before Christmas vacation, we were friends, but from the first day after the murder, she would not speak to me."

Not all the white students harassed their black schoolmates, but enough of them did to keep them on edge. One day, I was walking up the stairs as Louis Craft was coming down. A white boy on his way up elbowed Louis in the stomach. Although Louis could easily have knocked that boy down the stairs, he continued in his peaceful manner as if nothing had happened. As opposed to Louis's strategy of ignoring insults, Katie Davis would talk back when confronted with racial slurs. She didn't swear but stood her ground and didn't back down.[1]

About a block from the high school was a small restaurant, the "Blue Jay." Some students liked to go there for lunch or to just hang out. Pat told me:

> One day I was walking with several of the black students on our way home for lunch. As we passed the Blue Jay, we were hit by a rain of spit from several white boys. At first,, I didn't realize what had happened, but after we had gonc a little way, it dawned on me, and I was furious! I was no bigger than a minute, but I didn't care. I turned around and started back toward those white boys. The other black students tried to stop me, but I wasn't gonna to be stopped. I went right up to those boys standing in front of the Blue Jay and said, 'Who spit on me?' They didn't say anything, but after a while one of them started giggling. Then I was really mad. I worked up some spit in my own mouth and spit right in his face. He kicked me, but the police were standing by, saw what was happening, and stopped it.[2]

Despite the humiliation and hostility, all six black students graduated that spring. Pat Montjoy and Mable Bradford were among the 16 seniors who had earned memberships in the National Honor Society for character, scholarship, leadership, and service.[3]

Endnotes

1. Leatha Cranshaw Hale, Interview by author, February 1, 2010

2. Patricia Montjoy, Interview by author, May 20, 2005

3. *Enterprise-Courier,* May 30, 1957

# 14
# Graduation

The end of that difficult semester was marked by Commencement exercises held on Friday, May 24th, 1957 in the Charleston High School auditorium. Students and officials took their places on the stage as parents, relatives, and friends looked on.

There were 66 students in our senior class but more than 66 chairs on the stage during the ceremony. We students sat on folding chairs in assigned seats. As soon as we took our places, many white students who had been assigned to sit by a black student stood up, walked to the back of the stage, and sat in a row of extra chairs that had been put there. Because these chairs were already in place, it was obvious that this last protest had been planned in advance. Years later, I learned that a member of the school board had arranged for the row of empty chairs to be put there.[1]

When I got home that night, I received an "anonymous" phone call from a student who whispered, "Did you sit by a nigger at graduation?" I recognized the voice right away, a fellow student whom I thought I knew well.

It was noticeable that evening that when a white student came to the podium to receive his or her diploma, there was general applause, but when a black student stepped up, the applause came only from the black parents.[2]

* * *

Spring gave way to summer, and the town returned pretty much to normal. School opened in the fall without incident,[3] and the students of the Class of '57 had gone their separate ways. Thanksgiving and Christmas came and went with no more news of the search for the person who had raped June Castleberry and murdered Johnny Malugen.

## Endnotes

1. George Roberts, Interviews by author, December 27, 2009 and November 9, 2010

2. Leatha Crenshaw Hale, Interview by author, February 1, 2010

3. Charles Grau, Interview by author, 2017

# Part 3: 1958

## 15

## Two Boys, a Stolen Car, and a Gun

Joe Lester Slayton, seventeen, already had a record as a troubled and trouble-making youth when, in the summer of 1957, he was caught robbing the swimming pool office in Chaffee, Missouri. a small town 24 miles north of Sikeston. Already on parole for auto theft, he was sent to the Missouri State Training School for Boys in Boonville. At the time, he had been living in Chaffee with his uncle, Claude E. Slayton.

Slayton's mother and seven of his eight siblings, the youngest of whom was two months old, had moved to Chaffee in July 1957.[1] Joe Lester's father, Ralph Slayton, was incarcerated in the Missouri State Penitentiary serving a term for assault. The last record of Joe Lester's school attendance was for the 1956-1957 school year when he was reported to have been in the eighth grade. He was 16 years old.[2]

In February 1958, over a year after Johnny Malugen's murder, Joe Lester, while in Boonville, wrote a letter to his mother telling her what he had told no one else, that he knew who had killed Johnny Malugen. He also admitted to having been with the killer when the murder and rape occurred and that he had "shared the loot" from several robberies with the killer, but he denied active participation in the crimes. Slayton said he could not sleep until he told his mother what had happened. Slayton asked his mother to give his letter to Mr. H. E. "Tiny" Evans and to ask him to come to Boonville. Mr. Evans was a Special Agent with the Frisco Railway which had a station in Chaffee. Evans had befriended Joe Lester and visited him at the Training School before. In the pencil-written, unstamped letter which somehow reached his mother, Joe Lester also requested that his father come with Evans to Boonville. His father, Ralph Slayton, was still incarcerated in the penitentiary, and, of course, would not be released to make the trip.

Mrs. Slayton was unable to reach Evans, who was out of town, so she took the letter to Robert Driskell, the officer who had arrested Joe for the swimming pool robbery. Officer Driskell in turn took the letter to Scott County Sheriff John Dennis who immediately called Sikeston Police Chief Arthur Bruce. Dennis and Bruce called authorities in Boonville and arranged a meeting with Joe Lester and Mr. Pat Sweeney, Superintendent of the Missouri State Training School for Boys. They drove the 270 miles from Sikeston to Boonville, and when they arrived Mr. Sweeney met them and introduced them to Joe Lester Slayton.

Slayton told them that he had a friend, Lynn Wayne Hester, who had been in trouble for stealing cars in St. Louis. In December 1956, Hester's mother had sent him to Chaffee to live with his uncle, Ross Gregory. Slayton said that on the evening of the murder, he and Hester had stolen a car from Bryant's Machine Shop on the outskirts of Chaffee. Their intention was to drive toward Sikeston and find a filling station to rob. However, he said, the stations they passed were too well lighted and too busy to rob, so they went on to Sikeston and "drove around for a while." Their wandering led them to a dirt road on the edge of town where they saw and passed a parked car with a boy and a girl inside. Slayton recalled that Hester had said to him, "Let's go back there and take that girl away from that boy." Slayton responded, "That boy might be too big for us to kick around." Hester pointed to the pistol he had stolen from his uncle and said, "I'll use this on him if I have to!" Slayton said he didn't think that was a good idea, but Hester stopped the car anyway, got out, and walked back toward the car they had passed. Slayton stated, "I stayed inside the car." After waiting a few minutes inside the stolen car, he heard two shots, panicked, got out of the car, and ran away.

Slayton told the men that he thought Hester might be living with his mother, near St. Louis. Based on Slayton's account, law officials from Sikeston phoned and collaborated with officials in St. Louis where Hester's mother, Mrs. Modine Sloan, was found to be living in the St. Louis suburb of Wellston. So it was, that late Thursday afternoon, February 20, 1958, seven men stood at Mrs. Sloan's door on Myrtle Avenue in Wellston. Mrs. Sloan answered the knock at her door and greeted the men: Scott County Sheriff John Dennis, Sikeston Chief of Police Arthur Bruce, Scott County Prosecuting Attorney Weber Gilmore[3]; Detective Corporal Clarence Peetz and Detective Robert Green of the St. Louis Metropolitan Police Department; Corporal Roger Spreck and Patrolman William McKenna of the Wellston Police Department. Modine and Lynn Wayne had been eating supper when the men arrived. They had with them a fugitive warrant for the arrest of Lynn Wayne Hester with charges of murder and rape. With his mother looking on, Lynn Wayne was handcuffed and led from the house to a waiting police car. As he was escorted out, Hester demanded, "What are you doing that for? I ain't murdered nobody." In fact, he vehemently denied having any knowledge of the crime.

The officers took Lynn Wayne to the Wellston police station and then to the St. Louis Metropolitan Police Department where he was administered a lie detector test. The test suggested that he was not giving truthful answers to the questions he was asked. He spent the night in jail.[4]

## Endnotes

1. *The Daily Sikeston Standard,* February 21, 1958; *Enterprise-Courier,* February 27, 1958; *Chaffee Signal,* February 27, 1958

2. *Chaffee Signal,* February 27, 1958

3. (George) Weber Gilmore Sr. (1919-2002) was born in Charleston, Missouri, graduated from Columbus University in Washington, DC, and practiced law in Sikeston, Missouri for 50 years during which, in the 1950s, he served as Scott County Prosecuting Attorney. In 1958 Gilmore prosecuted Lynn Wayne Hester for the murder of Johnny Malugen. Later he moved to Benton, Kentucky. He was a major in the U. S, Army in the Pacific Campaign during World War II and was awarded the Bronze Star. He was a member of the First Christian Church of Sikeston. [*Southeast Missourian,* 5/7/02]

4.. *The Daily Sikeston Standard,* February 21, 1958; *Enterprise-Courier,* February 27, 1958; *Chaffee Signal,* February 27, 1958

# 16
# Confession

Around noon on Friday, February 21, 1958, the day after the arrest, the officers took Hester to Benton, the Scott County seat. That evening he was subjected to a thorough interrogation in the sheriff's office during which he would later tell authorities that Sheriff Dennis had "brought him two cheeseburgers, a glass of milk, and two sodas" and allowed him to call his mother. Hester continued to deny any involvement in the murder or rape but began to lose confidence when shown Joe Lester Slayton's signed statement. Just before midnight, Hester broke down and confessed to the murder but continued to deny having raped June Castleberry.

Hester signed a long and detailed confession, witnessed by Sheriff Dennis, Police Chief Bruce, Prosecuting Attorney, Gilmore, Chief Deputy Aubrey Michael,[1] Deputy Lillian Scherer, Mississippi County Sheriff Ernest Scott, and R. D. Clayton, a prominent citizen of Sikeston.

In his confession, Hester said he believed he was 18 years old and that he was born November 27, 1939 in Morehouse, Missouri, near Sikeston. Hester stated that in December of 1956 he had stolen a .32 caliber pistol from his uncle in Chaffee. Just after dark on Saturday, January 5, 1957, he and Joe Slayton stole a brown and cream colored '49 Ford coupe from Bryant's Machine Shop in Chaffee. With Slayton in the passenger seat, Hester drove the car to Sikeston. They ended up on a country road on the outskirts of town. On that road they passed a parked car with a couple in it. Hester drove three or four hundred yards farther and parked the (stolen] car. Continuing his story, he said, "We didn't have any money, so I took the pistol and walked back to the car to rob the couple." He said that when he opened the driver's door, the boy reached across the girl and grabbed a knife. At that point, Hester adamantly stated, "The boy came at me with the knife, and I shot." Hester said he had fired two shots: "the first missed but the second didn't." After I shot the boy, Hester recalled, "the girl screamed, and I ran back to the car and drove off." Slayton wasn't in the car, he said, so he went ahead and "drove around Sikeston for a while." He said that while in Sikeston he heard people talking about the murder and learned that the area was being searched for a black man who had committed the crime. Heading back to Chaffee, Hester saw Slayton walking along the highway and picked him up. They got back to Chaffee around 3:00 a.m., parked the car near the city disposal tanks, and spent the rest of the night at Hester's grandmother's house.

Hester said that on Sunday morning, the day after the murder, he went to town and bought a box of 410 gauge shotgun shells. Then he and Slayton went hunting. As they were returning home after hunting, Hester took the stolen pistol from his pocket and threw it into a deep ravine in a densely wooded area. Slayton asked him if he had done anything, and he answered, "I shot a man."[2]

The day after Hester's confession, Sheriff Dennis and Police Chief Bruce took Hester to Chaffee to show them the ravine into which he had thrown the pistol. The officers borrowed an army mine detector to aid with the search. A good number of Sikeston Auxiliary police and several citizens of the area joined the effort and searched all day for the pistol in a terrain thick with brush. The weapon was not found. Further searches were conducted in the days to come, but the gun was never recovered.

On Sunday, February 23, Sheriff Dennis and Police Chief Bruce took Hester to the scene of the crime. While there, Hester showed the officers where he had passed Johnny's car, where he parked the stolen car, how he walked back to Malugen's car, and how he remembered the shooting to have occurred. He also admitted, again, that he had shot Johnny Malugen but strongly denied having raped June Castleberry. After Hester had reviewed the details of the murder, the officers took him to the Sikeston police station.

June had moved to Memphis after graduating from Sikeston High School and was home visiting her parents when she learned that the man arrested for murdering Johnny was in custody. She requested an opportunity to confront the accused man and the police had promptly arranged a meeting at the police station.

Although June could not positively identify Hester as her assailant, she said he was about the same size as the man she remembered. She was, however, convinced that Hester was guilty when he calmly admitted that he had shot Johnny Malugen. June then accused him of assaulting her. Hester spat back, "If you say I attacked you, you are lying!," to which June responded, "You know you did it!" The accusations and denials continued in a heated fashion until the meeting was terminated.[3]

* * *

Hester's denial of having committed rape while admitting to murder remained, for the time being, a mystery. From the outset many details had been sketchy or even misleading. June's ability to identify her assailant had been a problem from the beginning. In an article *Enigma of the Extra Face*[4] which was written in 1958 for a publication *Official Detective Stories*, the author wrote: "Examined objectively, the girl had been unable to offer much. It was a dark night and at no time did she get a good look at the face of the man. He was about six feet tall, she said. The question of color was clouded by her insistence that something was different about his skin."

"June had said that her impression of his 'funny' skin was rooted in something she could not explain. She didn't know nor could she remember if she had touched the attackers face and got this impression or if she actually saw his skin."[5] Initially and throughout the investigation, June had maintained that her attacker wore a mask, had dark or unusual skin, and that she thought he was black. Never during the manhunt nor in the following months did authorities look for, or consider looking for, a man that fit Hester's description. Lynn Wayne Hester was, in fact, a *white* youth. He had blue eyes, brown hair, and was five feet eleven inches tall. While June's account of what her attacker did to her was detailed and accurate, the truth remained that she had not clearly seen him at all that night.[6]

On Tuesday, February 25, officers brought Hester to the Scott County Courthouse in Benton for arraignment before Magistrate

Court Judge Marshall Elmer Montgomery[8] who formally charged him with murder and rape. Attorney Eugene Munger[9] of St. Louis, a former resident of Scott County, was appointed to defend Hester at trial.

The courtroom was crowded with curious onlookers as the proceedings began. Hester again admitted that he had killed Malugen during an intended robbery but again denied having committed rape. He appeared calm, even unconcerned, despite the fact that Prosecuting Attorney Weber Gilmore declared that he would seek the death penalty. In fact, this attitude of seeming indifference had continued to characterize Hester's demeanor since his arrest the previous Thursday afternoon.[7]

A preliminary hearing was scheduled for Thursday, March 6 before Judge Montgomery in magistrate court at Benton. On that day, however, Hester's attorney, Eugene Munger,[8] filed an affidavit charging bias and prejudice and asked Judge Montgomery[9] to disqualify himself. In response, Judge Montgomery requested that Judge Erie Wright of New Madrid preside. Judge Wright agreed to do so, and Judge Montgomery postponed the hearing until Thursday March 13.

## Endnotes

1. Chief Deputy Aubrey Michael (1919-1989) was a self-employed farmer, sold real estate, and was the Scott County, Missouri Collector before becoming Chief Deputy Sheriff for the Scott County Sheriff's Department. He was an Army veteran, served in World War II, and was a member the American Legion where he was Commander of

Post 369. He was also a member of the Shriners of St. Louis and the Benton United Methodist Church. [*Southeast Missourian* 3/14/89]

2. *The Daily Sikeston Standard,* February 22, 1958; *Enterprise-Courier,* February 27, 1958

3 *The Daily Sikeston Standard,* February 24, 1958; *Enterprise-Courier,* February 27, 1958

4. The author possesses this article, *Enigma of the Extra Face,* but does not have the publication in which it appeared nor its exact date.

5. The above two consecutive quotes in consecutive paragraphs, each beginning and ending with quotations marks, are direct quotes from *Enigma of the Extra Face.* The first quote begins with the word "examined" and the second ends with "skin."

6. The physical description of Lynn Wayne Hester may be seen in a photograph in this book between the Epilogue and Historical Context: 1900-1950. He is standing between Weber Gilmore and Police Chief Arthur Bruce and is obviously white. Hester's Prison Parole Note in 1974 in the same series as the group photo is nearby and indicates that Hester had been a mechanic. This document was obtained on December 27, 2001 by the author from the Missouri Department of Corrections. In 1958, the *Chaffee Signal* said that Hester had dark or unusual skin.

7. *The Daily Sikeston Standard,* February 25, 1958

8. Eugene Marvin Munger (1896-1968) had been a resident of the St. Louis suburb of Brentwood after having lived in Bloomfield, Benton, and Chaffee, Missouri. He graduated from the Chicago Law School in 1922 and practiced law in Southeast Missouri and St. Louis until he died in 1968. Munger was a veteran of World War I and by the

end of it had achieved the rank of Captain. He served a term in the Missouri House of Representatives after having been elected in 1932.

9. *The Sikeston Daily Standard,* March 6, 1958

# 17
# A Guilty Conscience

Joe Lester Slayton had been closely observed since he had accused Hester of the murder and rape. Superintendent Sweeney and other officers had noticed that he appeared to be worried about something, as if he had a "load on his mind." On March 26, 1958, Sweeney called Joe Lester into his office and asked what was bothering him. During their talk, Slayton admitted that he, rather than Hester, had raped June Castleberry.

Superintendent Sweeney notified Sheriff Dennis and told him what Slayton had said. Then Dennis and Prosecuting Attorney Gilmore obtained from Judge Marshall Craig[1] a writ of habeas corpus which gave them the authority to bring Slayton to court if necessary. Dennis and Gilmore drove to Boonville where Slayton gave them his modified version of what had happened the night of the murder.[2]

The first part of Slayton's story was consistent with his original one and the one told by Hester. He said he was involved with Hester in stealing the car in Chaffee and was a passenger when Hester drove to Sikeston. He described the scene on the country road where Johnny's car was parked, how they had driven past the car with the couple inside and then parked the stolen car nearby. According to his original account, he had remained in the car when Hester got out and began to approach the Malugen car.

In this *second* version, however, Slayton said he left the stolen car and followed, unbeknownst to Hester, at a distance. He then stood out of sight behind Johnny's car and watched as Hester fired two shots. As soon as the shots were fired, Slayton said that Hester ran back in the direction of the car they had come in. At this point, June got out of Johnny's car and began screaming. Slayton said he immediately grabbed the girl, choked and slapped her into submission, then dragged her across a cotton field and raped her. He stated that after committing the act he had talked like a Negro and said he had to get back to St. Louis. He said the reason he had not admitted to raping June was because he felt ashamed.[2]

Slayton said that after assaulting the girl, he ran across the cotton field and railroad tracks, then across Salcedo Road to Highway 61 north of the North Y in Sikeston. From there, he ran and walked to the Delta Drive-in Theater where he caught a ride to the junction of Highways 61 and 55[3] near Morley.

He continued north by hitching another ride which dropped him off near the viaduct at Oran. He then walked to the first curve south of Chaffee. Coincidentally, just as he reached the curve past the viaduct, Hester was returning to Chaffee from Sikeston in the stolen car. There, he said, Hester saw him and picked him up.[4] Chaffee is 24 miles north of Sikeston, and Morley is half-way.

* * *

After hearing Slayton's rendition of the events surrounding the murder of Johnny Malugen, Sheriff Dennis and Prosecuting Attorney Gilmore took him to St. Louis for further questioning and a polygraph test. The test "showed convincingly" that he was telling the truth. Later in the day, Gilmore and Dennis took Slayton to Benton and filed charges in the juvenile division of Circuit Court. Given Slayton's confession, Gilmore announced that the rape charges against Hester would be dropped.

Having signed his confession, Slayton was formally arrested and brought before Judge M. E. Montgomery in magistrate court where he was arraigned and charged with the assault and rape of June Castleberry. Montgomery then appointed attorneys David Blanton[5] of Sikeston and Tom Arnold[6] of Benton to represent Slayton at his preliminary hearing on Tuesday, April 8. The day Slayton was arrested and charged, he was placed in the juvenile cell of the county courthouse in Benton. This cell, which was reserved for juvenile offenders and women prisoners, was not attached to the main jail but was a block away. Three nights later, shortly before midnight, on Sunday, April 6, two boys joined Slayton in the cell. Around 1:30 a.m., the boys disassembled a bunk bed and used part of it to pry a bar loose from the door, remove it, and then bend another bar just enough for a boy to slide through. Slayton and one of the boys escaped, but the other boy refused to leave. At 6:30 that morning, the jailer, Albert Rogers, went to the boys' cell, which was on the upper floor of the courthouse, and found just one boy. The boy told Rogers that the other two boys had told him they planned to sleep during the day and travel by night, robbing farmhouses.

A bulletin was released. In it, Slayton, a fair skinned white boy, was described as "the timid type, five feet six inches tall, weighing 140 pounds, and having blond hair." He was said to be wearing "blue denim trousers, a white shirt, a gray whipcord jacket, black leather shoes with a V cut in the heel, and a two-inch wide black belt.

He walked with a slight stoop." As it would turn out, Slayton did not rob any farmhouses but went straight to his grandfather's house in Chaffee. His grandfather, Able Francis Slayton, persuaded him to return to the jail and drove him there.[7]

* * *

Slayton's preliminary hearing, originally scheduled for April 8, was postponed several times because the defense attorneys had not had the opportunity to talk to June Castleberry who was living in Memphis. June and her twin, Jean, were working there as licensed practical nurses. On May 7, Slayton came before Judge Montgomery in magistrate court and waived a preliminary hearing. Two dozen spectators appeared at the hearing, and the case was transferred to Circuit Court where he would be tried as an adult. No bail was set, and Slayton remained in the Scott County jail awaiting trial.[8]

## Endnotes

1. Marshall M. Craig (1907-1998) graduated from the University of Missouri in 1930 and while there was captain of the Missouri Tigers basketball team. In 1930 he was selected first team All-American and in 1992 was inducted into the Missouri Basketball Hall of Fame. Marshall graduated from the University of Missouri Law School in 1932 and became an assistant U.S. attorney in St. Louis from 1937 to 1939. He later served as Mississippi County Prosecuting Attorney. He became a circuit judge of the 28th District in 1955 and was then appointed the first senior judge in Missouri and served four terms until 1979. Craig served eight years on the Sikeston Public Library

board, served as secretary of the United Way of Sikeston, was a former director and vice chairman of the Sikeston Industrial Development Council, and a former member of the Sikeston Public Schools Advisory Council. He was a longtime member of the Sikeston and Charleston Lions Clubs and past commander of several American Legion posts. He was a member of the First United Methodist Church where he had been a Sunday School teacher. He was also a member of the Masonic Lodge. Craig was an Eagle Scout and served as president of the SEMO Boy Scout Council and had been a worker for the Salvation Army. [*Southeast Missourian* 9/2/98]

2. *The Daily Sikeston Standard,* March 27, 1958; *Enterprise-Courier,* March 27, 1958

3. In the 1950s, State Highway 55 passed through Chaffee. When *Interstate* 55 was constructed, the name of State Highway 55 was changed to State Highway 77 which currently passes through Chaffee. *Interstate* 55, from New Orleans to Chicago, was begun in July 1957 and completed in September 1964.

4. *The Daily Sikeston Standard,* March 27, 1958; *Enterprise-Courier,* April 3, 1958

5. David Edgar Blanton (1908-1999) the youngest of seven children, was independent minded and stood up for his principles. As a young man he worked for a clothing store and 'borrowed' his way through the University of Missouri. When he returned to Sikeston he became a prominent lawyer and was elected Scott County Prosecuting Attorney. At the time, David's father, "C. L." Blanton, editor of the *Sikeston Standard,* made it clear that he was opposed to civil rights for "coloreds" and was noncommittal concerning lynching. Readers sometimes called him the "polecat," (a skunk like animal.) These attitudes

became a bone of contention between C. L. and his sons. Incidentally, David Blanton introduced the author's father to his mother in 1936.

6. Thomas Lee Arnold (1922-2013) served in World War II as a medic in France after the "D-Day," Normandy invasion in 1944. He was with the 44th Infantry Division, the unit that escorted the famed rocket scientist Dr. Wernher von Braun to allied custody. He learned fluent French and received the Bronze Star during his military service. He was a 1943 graduate of Southeast Missouri Teachers College (now Southeast Missouri State University) in Cape Girardeau. After the War, Thomas attended law school at the University of Missouri and graduated in 1948 on the GI Bill. Arnold then practiced law in Benton, the Scott County seat, and retired in 1994. Along with David Blanton he represented Joe Lester Slayton at his preliminary hearing on April 8, 1958. Arnold was involved in local and state Democratic causes. [*The Southeast Missourian* 4/28/13]

7.*The Missourian*, April 7, 1958; *Enterprise-Courier*, April 10, 1958

8. *The Daily Sikeston Standard*, May 7, 1958

# 18

# Hester's Trial

Hester's two-day trial began at 9:30 a.m. Friday, June 20, 1958 in Circuit Court in Benton, Missouri, with Judge Marshall Craig presiding. *The Daily Sikeston Standard* stated, "The Courtroom was packed to the doors with a throng of spectators drawn by the area's most celebrated murder trial in recent years, and it looks as though it will be a lengthy one." Weber Gilmore, assisted by Robert A. Dempster,[1] represented the State and squared off against Eugene Munger, the court-appointed defense lawyer.

Jury selection began Friday morning. Before the formal examination of the panel of prospective jurors began, four men were dismissed because of their views about the case. One of the four said he didn't believe in the death penalty. Another man declared that he could not form an opinion until the accused was "clearly proved innocent." Defense attorney Eugene Munger began the formal questioning of the panel after which Prosecuting Attorney Weber Gilmore completed the process. When Gilmore finished, twelve jurors acceptable to both lawyers had been selected.[2]

* * *

After jury selection, Mr. Gilmore began to lay out his case by recounting the events in the order in which they had occurred. Addressing the judge and jury he began:

"If it please the court and the jury, the State in this case shall prove by competent evidence and beyond a reasonable doubt that on January 5, 1957, June Castleberry had a date with the deceased Johnny Malugen, and the same evening Lynn Wayne Hester and his friend, Joe Lester Slayton, went to the outskirts of the city of Chaffee, Missouri, and obtained an automobile.

"The evidence will further show Gentlemen[3] of the Jury, that previous to this Saturday, January 5, 1957, the defendant, Lynn Wayne Hester and Joe Slayton had a conversation in connection with some stocking masks.

"The evidence will further show, Gentlemen, that at the special insistence and request of the defendant, Lynn Wayne Hester, his companion, Joe Slayton, did prepare at his home in Chaffee, Missouri that Saturday morning, two stocking masks. That when they met on Saturday evening, Joe Slayton gave Lynn Wayne Hester one mask, and Joe Slayton kept a mask himself.

"They left Chaffee and headed south on Route 55[4] toward Sikeston. Lynn Wayne Hester, somewhere between Chaffee, Missouri, and Morely, Missouri, exhibited to his companion, Joe Slayton, a .32 caliber revolver pistol, which he carried in his waistline.

"Lynn Wayne Hester, told his companion that they would knock off and rob a filling station on their way down to Sikeston, and they stopped and canvassed several filling stations. They stopped at the Grant City Oil Station in Scott County on Route 61 and purchased $2.00 worth of gas. They discussed robbing these places but found them too well lighted and too active. When they got to Sikeston, they drove around a while and then crossed the Frisco Railroad tracks on the northwest side of Sikeston and drove north up a country lane.

"At about the same time, June Castleberry and her boyfriend, Johnny Malugen, had left the theater where she worked, gone to a drive-in, had a cup of hot chocolate, and then had driven north of Sikeston on 61 and come around and were parked on this road, headed in a southerly direction, where the defendant and his companion were going north.

"The defendant and his companion went around the automobile which contained June Castleberry and her companion, Johnny Malugen. As they passed this automobile the defendant, Hester, said to his companion, Slayton, 'See that girl in that car?' They went around and Hester stopped the car and told his companion, Joe Slayton, 'Let's go back there and rob them and take the boy's girlfriend.'

"At that time, Joe Slayton said to the defendant, Hester, 'That boy might be too big for us to kick around.' The defendant, Hester, pointing to the gun he then carried in his belt, said, 'If they do, I'll use this on them.'

"These two young men then put on their cotton masks, and Slayton said to defendant Hester, 'I'll wait in the car.'

"The defendant then got out of the car and walked down the road to the automobile, which contained June Castleberry and her friend, Johnny Malugen.

"After defendant Hester got some distance from his automobile, his companion, Slayton, got out of the car and followed him. Slayton could see his companion, Hester, the defendant at all times. Hester walked up to the left front door. the driver's door, and immediately afterward the defendant's companion,

Slayton, walked up to the right rear of the car containing June Castleberry and Johnny Malugen.

"The evidence will further show that as Joe Slayton was standing at the right rear of the automobile, he observed his companion, Hester, pull open the driver's door of the automobile, holding the pistol in his right hand, and tell the boy, Johnny Malugen, to get out of the car.

"At that time Johnny Malugen closed the door of the car. Lynn Wayne Hester pulled the door back open. At that time Lynn Wayne Hester said to Johnny, 'If you don't get out of there, I'll kill you.'

"At that time, Johnny Malugen said to his girlfriend, June Castleberry, 'Hand me the knife out of the glove compartment.' June Castleberry did reach into the glove compartment for the knife, and before she could get the knife from the glove compartment and into the hands of her companion, the defendant did shoot Johnny Malugen.

"A bullet grazed the lower part of the upper left arm, went into his left chest cavity and lodged in his heart.

"The defendant, Hester, then turned and fled, got into the car he had driven there, drove off and left his companion, Slayton.

"Johnny Malugen was dead when the officers arrived at the scene later that night.

"At approximately 1:00 or 2:00 in the morning Slayton by various rides and hitchhiking worked his way back to Chaffee, Missouri and met Hester. They went to the defendant's grandmother's home and when they got there, the defendant's Aunt was waiting up for them and chastised them for being out so late. They went to bed, got up the next morning and went hunting, and while they were hunting the defendant Hester took out the pistol he had used the previous evening and threw it into a rugged ravine and said to his companion, Slayton, 'If you ever tell, you'll get the same thing the boy at Sikeston got.'

"On Thursday, the 20th day of February, 1958, more than thirteen months following the murder and after a long an arduous manhunt, the Sheriff of this county, John Dennis, accompanied by me, Arthur Bruce, Chief of Police of the City of Sikeston, two Wellston, Missouri Police Officers, and two Officers from the Police Department of the City of St. Louis went to Wellston to the home of Modine Sloan, the mother of the defendant, Hester, who had been living with her. The officers had with them a warrant charging Lynn Wayne Hester with murder in the first degree.

"They took into custody the defendant, Lynn Wayne Hester. When the handcuffs were put on Hester, he said, 'What are you doing that for? I ain't killed nobody.'

"Thereafter in the Wellston Police Station, the defendant was told what he was charged with and advised of his rights. The next day, Friday, February 21st, 1958, he was brought to the Scott County Sheriff's office in Benton, Missouri. Hester was not mistreated in any way, shape, or fashion, not promised anything, and given no encouragement. He was informed that anything he might say could be used against him later in court.

"Upon reaching Benton, Missouri, the defendant, while talking to the Sheriff and his chief deputy, Aubrey Michael, did voluntarily admit to the officers that he was the one who had shot Johnny Malugen.

"On the morning of Saturday, February 22, 1958, the defendant agreed to go to Chaffee, Missouri, with the Sheriff of Scott County and the Chief of Police of Sikeston. They went to Chaffee and picked up Chief Masterson of Chaffee and drove down to the defendant's grandmother's home.

"The Sheriff of Scott County allowed the defendant to go in and talk to his grandmother, his aunt, and his mother (who had come down from St. Louis to be with her family). Chief Bruce of Sikeston and Chief Masterson of Chaffee accompanied him into his grandmother's home and while there, in the presence of this mother, his aunt, and his grandmother, the defendant, Lynn Wayne Hester, again admitted to his relatives and mother that he had shot Johnny Malugen.

"Later, he went with the authorities and took them to the rugged ravine where he remembered having thrown the pistol, the murder weapon.

"On Sunday, February 23, the defendant agreed to come to Sikeston, Missouri, with Sheriff Dennis and while at Sikeston, Missouri, and in the presence of June Castleberry and her mother, did admit to June Castleberry that he was the man who had shot her boyfriend.

"Now, Gentlemen of the Jury, if the State proves all these facts as I have outlined them to you, which we feel we can, and beyond a reasonable doubt, then Gentlemen, we expect you to find the DEFENDANT GUILTY OF MURDER IN THE FIRST DEGREE AND ACCESS THE EXTREME PENALTY OF DEATH. I THANK YOU"

* * *

The first witness called was Joe Lester Slayton who said he had known Lynn Hester since December 1956. Slayton's story was essentially the same as that he had told the previous February when in Boonville. He said that before driving to Sikeston on the night of the murder, he and Hester had made two masks from women's brown stockings at the home of Hester's grandmother, Mrs. Rose Steinkamp. After arriving in Sikeston, they drove to the west end of town and onto a farm road parallel to the Frisco railway tracks. They were going north on that road when they passed a car with a couple in it. They continued for another 400 feet or so, parked the car they had come in, and put on their masks. Hester got out and started walking toward the car they had passed. After remaining in the car for a short time, Slayton said he followed Hester and watched the struggle between Hester and Malugen. He said he heard two shots at which time Hester ran back toward the car they had come in and drove away. Having been left behind, Slayton said he made his way back to Chaffee and that he and Hester spent the night in Hester's grandmother's house. The two of them went hunting the next day, and Hester threw away the pistol he had used the night before.

The next witness was June Castleberry. She stated that she had known Malugen for about eight months and had dated him occasionally. At 9:30 on the night of January 5, 1957, Johnny picked her up after her shift at the Rex Movie Theater and drove to the South Y (a place where two highways met) where they had soft drinks at a small restaurant there. From there, they drove north to Salcedo Road, crossed the Frisco railway tracks, and then turned south on a field road. They had been parked for about ten minutes, she said, when a masked man whom she thought was a Negro approached the driver's side of the car. She recounted the details of the murder and said that she was then criminally assaulted by the man she thought had shot Johnny. She told how she had run across the cotton field to the Frisco tracks and down the country road to North Street where she encountered Mr. and Mrs. Henry Cooper who offered to help her.

The last witness called on the first day of the trial was Dr. A. B. Smith who testified that he had examined the victim's body at about 11:30 p.m. the night of the murder and again early the next morning. He said he found a lead bullet lodged in the base of Johnny's heart.

The first witness to testify on the second day of the trial was the Scott County Chief Deputy Sheriff Aubrey Michael who said that he was present when Hester was arrested and again the next day when he was taken to Benton. He said Hester denied any knowledge of the murder until after extensive questioning when he was confronted with Slayton's written and signed statement which detailed the events that occurred on the night of the murder. The Deputy testified that two days after his confession, Hester made a verbal statement that went into detail about how he had stolen the pistol from his uncle with the intention of using it in a robbery.

Michael remained on the stand and was cross-examined by defense attorney Munger about the conditions under which Hester made and signed his confession. In response, Michael said that he had not coerced or threatened Hester in any way and had not promised him anything.[5]

Prosecuting Attorney Gilmore read Hester's confession to the jury and presented it to the court as evidence. The written statement may be seen below:

> "I, LYNN WAYNE HESTER, having been duly warned that I do not have to make any statement and that anything I might say hereafter can be used against me in Court, possessing all my mental faculties, and being the age of 18 years, do hereby make the following statement to Sheriff John Dennis, Chief Deputy Aubrey Michael, both of Benton, Scott County, Missouri; Chief of Police Arthur Bruce, of Sikeston, Scott County, Missouri; and

Sheriff J. Ernest Scott, of Charleston, Mississippi County, Missouri, voluntarily knowing the same to be true, without threats, or duress or promises of any character whatsoever having been made.

"My name is Lynn Wayne Hester, and I am 18 years of age. I was born on November 27, 1939. I live with my mother, Modine Sloan, and stepfather, John James Sloan, at 6434 Myrtle, Wellston, Missouri.

"Sometime in December 1956, I went out to my uncle's, Ross Gregory, who lives outside the city limits of Chaffee. There was no one at home and I went in the house. I went down there with the intention of getting a gun. My uncle had a .32 pistol. I knew where he kept it, and I went in and got it from under the pillow on his bed. I kept the gun for a while and then on the evening of January 5th, 1957, me and Joe Slayton stole a car from Bryant's Machine Shop in Chaffee. This was a '49 Ford, brown bottom with cream top.

"It was sometime after dark. Me and Joe Slayton drove down to Sikeston. I did the driving. We rode around a while and then drove through Sikeston and crossed some railroad tracks on to a road west, straight down these railroad tracks. We passed a car that was parked on this road and drove on about 300 or 400 feet and stopped. We talked about them having some money and we didn't have any, so I went back to this car with the purpose of robbing them. I went to the right side of this car and opened the door. The boy in the car under the steering wheel jumped across the girl out at me with a knife.[6]

"When I saw him start to come at me, I pulled the trigger on the gun which I had previously stolen from my uncle in Chaffee. I fired this gun twice. The girl screamed and I ran back to the car and got in and I drove around trying to find my way out of there and finally did and then went home.

"While this was happening, Slayton had left the car and had taken off across the field. I drove around for a while and then I headed for Chaffee. When I got there, I seen Joe walking out of his uncle's or grandmother's house. I don't know which one it was. I picked him up and we drove back in a field on a ditch. We left the car there and we both went to my grandmother's house.

"When I went to bed that night, I put the pistol under my pillow. When we got to my grandmother's, it was approximately 3:30 or later Sunday morning, January 6. We got up around 11:30 or 12:00 noon Sunday and ate and I went downtown and bought some shells for a 410 and we went hunting. After we got back, we went up on the hill east of the Frisco Round House where their water tower is and when we got on top of this hill, I threw the gun down the hill. I asked Slayton not to tell anybody. He said he wouldn't.

"We messed around quite a bit out in the woods and then went home. I stayed home that evening and night. Slayton asked me if I had done anything. I told him what I had done. That I had shot a man.

"During the time that I was driving around, I drove on past Chaffee to the Diversion Channel Bridge, turned around and drove back to Blomeyer. I kept driving back and forth up the road until I noticed that my gas tank was almost empty and that's when I headed back to Chaffee and picked up Joe Slayton.

"I have promised to go with the officers later this morning to show them where I threw the pistol and help them find it. During the questioning Sheriff Dennis brought me two cheeseburgers, a glass of milk, and two sodas. Sheriff Dennis let me call my mother twice before we left St. Louis and told me I could call her any time tonight that I wanted to."

The above statement was made in the presence of John Dennis, Sheriff, Scott County, Missouri, Chief Deputy Sheriff Aubrey Michael, of Benton, Missouri, Chief of Police Arthur Bruce, of Sikeston, Missouri, Sheriff J. Ernest Scott, of Charleston, Missouri, R. D.Clayton of Sikeston, Missouri and Lillian Scherer, Deputy Sheriff of Scott County.

"I have read the above statement, consisting of 2 pages, of my own free will and accord, without fear or intimidation, or promise of reward, and acknowledge the same to be true correct to the best of my knowledge."

Signed: Lynn Hester

WITNESSES:
John Dennis
Arthur Bruce
J. E. Scott
Aubrey Michael
R. D. Clayton
Lillian Scherer

When Sikeston Police Chief Arthur Bruce was called to the stand, he testified that on Sunday, February 23, Hester had led the officers to the scene of the crime, reenacted the crime, and again admitted having committed it. Chief Bruce also testified that later that same day at the Sikeston police station, Hester had admitted to June Castleberry and her mother, Estel Demaris, that he had shot Johnny Malugen.

Sheriff Dennis, a witness for the State, reiterated much of the testimony that previous witnesses had given. He also said that in Chaffee, on the way to look for the murder weapon, he and Hester had stopped at the home of Hester's uncle, Ross Gregory, where

Hester told his uncle that he had stolen his pistol and used it to shoot Malugen. In addition, Sheriff Dennis said that he had seen Dr. A. B. Smith extract the bullet from Johnny's heart.

Mr. and Mrs. Henry Cooper were the next witnesses. Mr. Cooper testified that at about 10:30 p.m. on January 5,1957 while stopped at the railroad crossing on North Street in a truck tractor belonging to his employer, he and his wife heard a girl's frantic screams and looked and saw June Castleberry running toward them. When he asked how he could help, and what was wrong, the girl had answered that "some Negro" had shot her boyfriend and then had assaulted her. It was a very cold night, he said, but the girl was wearing neither shoes nor coat. He went downtown, notified the police, and went with them to the crime scene. He saw the girl's shoes and coat in the car.

Mrs. Cooper testified that the girl, June Castleberry, had remained in the truck tractor and that she, Mrs. Cooper, stopped and called June's mother who came and took her daughter to the Delta Community Hospital.

Hester's grandmother, Rose Steinkamp, and his aunt, Edith Rook, both testified that they had asked Hester if he had committed the crime, and he said, "That's what they say."

Hester's uncle, Ross Gregory, testified that Hester had *not* stolen a pistol from him and that he had never owned one.

Defense attorney Munger then called Hester to the witness stand. Hester said that until he was arrested in St. Louis, he had never heard of Johnny Malugen. He disavowed his signed confession and denied everything he had admitted. When Munger asked why he had signed the confession, Hester said the officers had worn him down by talking to him for five or six hours, had beaten him with their hands and with a folded magazine, and that they had written the confession themselves, then forced him sign it. He did admit, however, that he had gone to Chaffee with the officers to look for a pistol and then to Sikeston with them to the crime scene. He said, however, that *he* had not taken the officers to the crime scene, but that *they* had taken him and that he had never been there before. Hester denied having told June Castleberry at the police station that he had shot Malugen.

Sheriff Dennis and Aubrey Michael were recalled to the stand and denied having hit Hester with anything. These were the last witnesses, and Judge Craig announced a one-hour recess.

* * *

After the court convened, defense attorney Eugene Munger spoke for 45 minutes urging the jury to declare Hester "not guilty." He carefully reviewed how Hester had denied ever having heard of Johnny Malugen until he was arrested for his murder. He repeated how Hester had disaffirmed any statement he had made connecting himself to the murder and stressed that he had disavowed his written confession. He asked the jury to recall Hester's having felt coerced into signing it. Lastly, Munger underscored Hester's statement that the officers had taken him to the crime scene rather than his having taken them.

The *Daily Sikeston Standard* described Munger's closing statement as "eloquent."

Prosecuting Attorney Weber Gilmore made the closing statement for the State. He pointed out how the statements by the witnesses dovetailed with each other and emphasized the testimony given by Joe Lester Slayton and June Castleberry. He underscored the verbal and written confessions of Lynn Wayne Hester. Both Gilmore and Dempster, who was assisting him, asked for the death penalty.

* * *

The jury retired to their chambers and after eating dinner deliberated for 30 minutes. At 7:24 the jury foreman presented the judge with their verdict:

> We, the jury, find Lynn Wayne Hester Guilty of murder in the first degree and assess his punishment as confinement in the Missouri State Penitentiary for the remainder of his natural life.[7]

When the verdict was announced Hester's mother, Modine Sloan, who had been close to her son during the entire trial, became hysterical and several women friends and relatives had tears in their eyes. Hester, himself showed no emotion at all.

Following its account of the trial, the Charleston newspaper, *Enterprise-Courier,* after a cursory study of court records, stated that most prisoners given a life sentence do not spend the rest of their lives in prison. It estimated that Hester would serve 15 to 20 years.[8]

Prosecuting Attorney Gilmore's son, George Weber Gilmore Jr, told the author that he had been in the courtroom during Hester's trial in 1958 but was not completely convinced that Hester was guilty. George was ten years old at the time.[9]

Hester appealed the verdict and his sentence to the Missouri Supreme Court. The case was heard on February 8, 1960. A detailed and concise account of the crime, the evidence, case law relevant to the crime, and an explanation of legal procedures were clearly explained.

The conclusive document can be seen below:

> The appeal, STATE of Missouri, Respondent v LYNN WAYNE HESTER, appellant No. 47318. Represented by Eugene M. Munger.
>
> The appellant was represented by counsel, he was present throughout the trial and when sentenced there was allocution and upon the record before the court there is no error, and the judgment is therefore affirmed.[10]

Translation: Hester's appeal was denied.

## Endnotes

1. Robert A. Dempster (1912-1995) was a philanthropist and civic leader in Sikeston, Missouri who practiced law there for 59 years -- from 1934 to 1993. He graduated from the University of Missouri Law School in 1934 and during his senior year was elected city attorney of Sikeston. For many years he was a major benefactor of Southeast Missouri State University in Cape Girardeau and helped to establish the Southeast Missouri University Foundation. Over the years the foundation raised millions of dollars for the university. Dempster's wife, Lynn, was a member of the school's Board of Regents while Robert funded the construction of an auditorium and a Hall of Nursing. In addition to his gifts to Southeast Missouri State University, Dempster made many financial contributions to his alma mater, the University of Missouri in Columbia. A major portion of

these contributions went to its law school of which he was a trustee. He was appointed to the University's Board of Curators in 1978 and during his time on the Board he was chairman of its finance committee. While in Sikeston Dempster helped to fund the construction of the Missouri Delta Medical Center's rehabilitation complex in Sikeston. He founded the Security National Bank of Sikeston and was appointed to the Board of Trustees of Scarritt College in Nashville, Tennessee. In 1942 Dempster became an officer in the Navy and spent two and a half years on the Pacific Island of Okinawa during World War II. He left the Navy with the rank of lieutenant commander. Dempster was a member of the First United Methodist of Sikeston and was involved in the development of the Wesley United Methodist Church. [*The Southeast Missourian* 3/26/95]

2. *The Daily Sikeston Standard,* June 20, 1958

3. To improve the clarity and readability of the remainder of Gilmore's opening statement. phrases such as "If it please the court," "beyond a reasonable doubt," and "the evidence will further show, Gentlemen" have been omitted from further quotes. For the same reason. a few explanatory phrases have been added.

4. In the 1950s, State Highway 55 passed through Chaffee. When *Interstate* 55 was constructed, the name of State Highway 55 was changed to State Highway 77 which currently passes through Chaffee. Interstate 55, from New Orleans to Chicago, was begun in July 1957 and completed in September 1964

5. *The Daily Sikeston Standard,* June 21, 1958

6. In his written confession, Hester stated:
a) "I went to the *right* side of this car and opened the door" and

b) "The boy in the car under the steering wheel jumped *across* the girl out at me with a knife." (Italics mine)
c) Both Joe Slayton and June Castleberry, however, stated that Hester had gone to the *left* side of the car, which was the driver's side.
d) Had this detail of Hester's written confession, that he had gone to the *right* side of the car, been true, it could have been used as a self-defense argument. It involved Malugen jumping toward Hester with a weapon, the knife, before Hester "pulled the trigger." This claim, however, was never mentioned in court by either attorney.

7. *The Daily Sikeston Standard,* June 23, 1958; *Enterprise-Courier,* June 26, 1958

8. *Enterprise-Courier,* June 26, 1958

9. George Weber Gilmore Jr., Interview by author, 2012

10. VersuLaw, copyright 1997; Justia Co. copyright 2015•

# 19
# Slayton's Fate

Joe Lester Slayton was arrested for the rape of June Castleberry and confined to the Scott County Jail on March 26, 1958.[1] He had testified at Hester's trial on June 21, 1958,[2] and on September 6, 1958 came before Judge Craig in Circuit Court for his own hearing. He was represented by Harry C. Blanton[3] and Roy "Rough" Hough,[4] his court-appointed attorneys, and at his hearing, pled guilty to the charge of rape. Judge Craig sentenced him to 15 years in the Missouri State Penitentiary.[5]

After having spent six weeks in the penitentiary, Slayton astonished prison officials and everyone else involved in his case when he told them that he himself, not Hester, had killed Johnny Malugen! Prison officials told him to cool down for 24 hours before he signed any confession and warned him that if he were convicted of murder he could be sentenced to life in prison or even death in the gas chamber. Ignoring this warning, Slayton signed a confession the next day. He said he had been thinking about Hester spending his life in prison "for something I done."

In this confession Slayton said that on the night of January 5, 1957, when he and Hester had passed Malugen's car and parked on the country road, Hester was in the back seat of the stolen car "sleeping off a drunk." Slayton said he reached into the back seat, got Hester's gun, walked to Malugen's car, and shot him. After committing the murder, he said, he drove back to Hester's grandmother's house where the two spent the night. The next morning Slayton said he threw the pistol into a Frisco railroad car, and told Hester that he, Hester, had committed the murder, and Hester believed him.

Slayton had already told two different stories of what happened the night of the murder. Nobody associated with apprehending or convicting the two boys believed Slayton's new story. Sheriff Dennis said, "Hester had to be the boy who did it because he reenacted the crime just three days after he was arrested." Police Chief Bruce, Deputy Michael, Prosecuting Attorney Gilmore, and Attorney Robert Dempster all agreed that Slayton's latest version of the story was highly unlikely. Another reason for their skepticism was that immediately after Slayton had signed his "confession" of having murdered Malugen, he was taken to the State Highway Patrol Headquarters in Jefferson City where a polygraph test was administered and suggested that he was lying.[6]

Slayton escaped from the Missouri State Penitentiary on November 4, 1958 but was apprehended four days later and returned to prison. He then served sentence until sometime in 1966 when he was paroled. During his parole period, he was arrested and convicted of second degree burglary and sentenced to three more years. Records from the Missouri State Penitentiary indicate that in January 1970, he was again paroled, apparently for the last time.[7] There is little information about Slayton after 1970 except that records from the Social Security Administration suggested that he was still living in 2010.[8]

Given Slayton's history, one might wonder what he had been doing during the 50 years since he was paroled in 1970. That is a long time for a man with no self-discipline or sense of direction to be "running loose" unsupervised. Could he have found a job good enough to allow him to focus on something beyond his next meal or a place to sleep? How much time had he spent in jail? He had already escaped from the Benton, Missouri County Jail in April 1958 and from the Missouri State Penitentiary in November 1958. He appears to have been a Houdini without a cause and no idea where he was going or why.

Joe Lester's father, Ralph Slayton, had been in the Penitentiary for assault when Joe Lester was a teenager and would not have been a good role model for responsible living.

The Social Security Administration's 2010 Census report indicating that Joe Lester was presumably living in 2010 gives us little information beyond the fact that he was probably not dead. To me, the author, it suggests that nobody, or at least no public official, knew anything at all about him. He could have been anywhere, living or dead.

Endnotes

1. *Enterprise-Courier*, March 27, 1958; *The Daily Sikeston Standard*, March 27, 1958

2 *The Daily Sikeston Standard*, June 21, 1958

3. Harry Cullen Blanton (1891-1973) graduated third in his class of 258 from the Georgetown University Law School in 1914 and then became a prominent lawyer in Sikeston, Missouri for the next 50

years. He was appointed by President Franklin Roosevelt to the position of U. S. Attorney for the Eastern District of Missouri and served there from 1934 to 1947. In 1918 he was inducted into the Army and served briefly in an administrative capacity until the end of the War. Blanton was very active in the American Legion for 53 years. He was part of the Scott County Democratic Central Committee from 1920 to 1928. Blanton was later elected to the Southeast Missouri Boy Scout Council and was a member of the Kiwanis Club, Chamber of Commerce, Knights of Columbus, and the St. Francis Xavier Catholic Church. This brief note barely scratches the surface of Blanton's accomplishments and awards during his interesting and productive lifetime. He and his wife, Maureen, raised four sons and four daughters. [*The Sikeston Standard*, 3/20/73] [Special to the Missourian]

4. Roy Finley Hough (1925-1979) joined the Army Air Corps and was ready to go into combat just as World War II ended. After an Honorable Discharge from the military, he studied law at Vanderbilt University and graduated in 1951. After he passed the Bar, he practiced law with Robert Dempster in Sikeston, Missouri for three years before going into private practice. In addition to law, Roy loved farming and owned a farm south of Morehouse, Missouri. He married Rosalie Marilyn Eddy in 1947 and had four children: Sandra Lee, John Edgar, David Finley, and Janet Ann. [source: David and Janet Hough 4/3/20]

5 *The Daily Sikeston Standard,* September 8, 1958; *Chaffee Signal,* September, 10, 1958; *Enterprise-Courier,* October 1, 1958

6. *The Daily Sikeston Standard,* December 30, 1958

7. Prison discharge note obtained by the author in 2004 from the Missouri Department of Corrections.

8. Sharon Sanders. Librarian/historian for the Cape Girardeau, Missouri newspaper, *Southeast Missourian,* Interview by author, 2012.

# 20

# What Became of Them?

What became of those who played central roles in the events recorded in this book? Beginning in 2014, through phone calls, letters, and interviews, I found answers to most of these questions.

After **Coach Dee Bonner** completed his coaching career at Charleston High School, he established a career in the insurance business, first in Charleston, Missouri and then in Memphis, Tennessee.[1] His death, about 2007, was attributed to cancer.

A good many years after she graduated from Charleston High School, **Mable Bradford,** now Robinson, recalled verbally and in writing many of her experiences since then. She wrote: "Desegregation enabled me and my black classmates to acquire the skills we needed to be competitive in the work force and to have more meaningful and rewarding lives. None of us black students stayed in the area after graduation, but some of us came back for our twentieth high school class reunion. One of our white classmates, Jane Banta, had called Pat Montjoy and told her about the reunion, and Pat called me. Pat and I were close, and I'm the Godmother of her son. In the fall of 1957, after graduating from Charleston High School, I began my first year of college at Howard University in Washington, DC.

"After two years at Howard, I transferred to Genesco University, part of the State Universities of New York (SUNY) and in 1962, graduated with a double major: Elementary Education and Special Education. Some years later, I obtained a Master of Education degree from Hofstra University which qualified me to teach English as a Second Language. I was the first African American to teach in the all white Northport School System and taught there for five years. Northport is a wealthy, upscale village on the north shore of Long Island in New York state. I was surprised to find that some black parents in Northport did not want their children in school with other black children and sent them to private schools. While teaching in the predominantly white Long Island neighborhoods, I often went to Harlem on weekends to visit my uncle.

"Near the end of my teaching career, I earned a certificate of administration. In 2002, after working in supervisory roles for two years, I retired. I didn't like administrative work because you had to be 'in a posse' with people who did things I didn't believe in. Altough I'm now retired (2014), I'm working part time for the Westbury School District.

"I have a daughter, Alma, who teaches in an elementary school in Atlanta.

"We are close and visit frequently.

"I'm active in the United Methodist Church, serve on the church board and on several committees. I volunteer with organizations dedicated to improving the lives and long-term prospects of children."

These include Delta Sigma Theta, Chums, and Sisters of the Arts. Mable has an unstoppable sense of humor. She said, "Just to see what it was like, I took a job in a business on Seventh Avenue in Manhattan. Things moved so fast in that part of town that after three months, I decided to 'get off the train.' In addition to the frantic pace of life there, I barely made enough money to pay for my round trip from Westbury to Manhattan and back. It was crazy. I'll tell you, if you can get through New York, you can get through anywhere. No, if you can get through Charleston, you can get through anywhere."[2]

**June Castleberry** married David Hart, a Missouri State Highway Patrolman. The couple lived in Springfield, Missouri, raised one son, two daughters, and had four grandchildren.[3] David Hart served on the Board of Directors of the Stars and Stripes Museum in Bloomfield, Missouri.[4]

June died on August 13, 1997[5], and David died some ten years later.[6]

**Louis Craft** moved to Los Angeles and was working for the government when he was sent on a secret mission to Turkey. Louis's mother, Vera, told John Goodin that after Louis returned to Los Angeles, he was mysteriously murdered. The case was never solved. John Goodin told me that there was hearsay that Louis's murder was arranged by the CIA at the behest of the State Department and that it had to do with Louis's trip to Turkey. To me this whole thing sounds outlandish and more like a James Bond novel than fact, but weird things have happened in this crazy world, especially during wartime, and Louis *was* murdered. John Goodin who shared these rumors with me told me not to share them with anybody, for fear of his own safety, but I did share them in this book because John is now deceased and out of danger.[7]

Louis's friend, Adam Holman, said that Louis was the type of guy who had self-control, got his lessons as he was supposed to, and worked hard at whatever he was doing. He loved basketball. He wasn't the best player but was always eager to do his part. He was honest, respectful, and humble. Louis was from a good family and liked people.[8]

**Leatha Crenshaw,** now Hale, went to Lincoln University in Jefferson City, Missouri, married, and had two daughters who provided her with two grandchildren. One of her daughters was single and died at age 28. The other daughter lives in Valpariso, Indiana. Leatha then moved to Chicago where she studied accounting at a Chicago Loop College and then at the University of Indiana Northwest. Leatha worked as an accountant for 26 years and ended her career as an Internal Revenue Agent in Chicago. She now lives in Gary, Indiana.[9]

**Willie Curtis** retired from the United States Air Force after 21 years of service. He then earned a doctoral degree in political science from the University of Delaware, graduating in 1983. He taught at the University of Wisconsin-Park Side from 1984 to 1989 and then at St. Cloud State University in Minnesota from 1989 to 1992. While at St. Cloud State, he received the Distinguished Teacher Award and the Outstanding Contribution Award. In 1992 he accepted a position as Associate Professor at the United States Naval Academy in Annapolis, Maryland.

Relevant to his responsibilities at the Academy, he took training at the Naval War College, the United States Air Force War College, and the Johns Hopkins School for Advanced International Studies. He served in many capacities including Consultant to the Department of Defense.

After a class reunion, forty or so years after graduating from Charleston High School, Willie was the Grand Marshal of the Dogwood Azalea Festival Parade in Charleston.[10]

As soon as **Katie Davis** graduated from Charleston High School in 1958, she moved to Gary, Indiana with her mother who had family there. That same year, Katie married Chris Oliver of Charleston, Missouri who at the time was in the military. The couple had four children, three of whom live in Gary and the other in Valpariso, Indiana, about 30 miles southeast of Gary. For many years Katie owned a beauty shop in her home and was a licensed beautician.[11]

The last time I spoke with her, in 2019, she was feisty and outspoken. She died of a stroke on March 7, 2019 and was buried on March 8, 2019 in Gary. Her funeral services were conducted at the Powell-Coleman Funeral Home.[12]

**Lynn Wayne Hester** was paroled in January 1973.[13] and since then had lived in the St. Louis area and in the Ozark Mountains of southeastern Missouri. Most recently he had lived in Doniphan, Missouri. I telephoned his home on June 20, 2010. A man answered the phone, and I asked him if Lynn was home. He said, "No, he died early this month." I asked the young man if he was a relative or a friend of the family. He said he was engaged to marry Lynn's daughter.

"Well then," I said, "You will be Lynn's son-in-law, right?" He replied, "I hope to be." He said Lynn's daughter was thirty-two years old and an only child. "Is Lynn's wife home?" I asked. He said she was out but would be back in a half-hour or 45-minutes. I told him I would call back in an hour. After a half-hour, Mrs. Hester called me. After I gave her my condolences, I told her my name and that I was writing a book about Johnny Malugen's murder. I explained that I wanted to learn more about Lynn. Mrs. Hester responded, "He got the rap but didn't do it." She also said in no uncertain terms that she didn't want me writing any book.[14]

According to the Edwards Funeral Home in Doniphan, Missouri, Lynn Wayne Hester died of cancer at the local hospital on June 4, 2010.[15]

The day after I spoke with Mrs. Hester, I called Johnny Malugen's niece, Diane LaCroix, and told her about my conversation with Lynn's wife and her denial that Lynn had killed Johnny. Diane said, "Well, if that helps their family get on with their lives, more power to them."[16]

I spoke to **Adam Holman** by phone, and he sent me a letter with family photographs. He said that following his graduation from Charleston High School in 1956, he enrolled at Tuskeegee Institute in Alabama. After two years at Tuskeegee, he transferred to Lincoln University in Jefferson City, Missouri where he graduated in 1960 with a B.S. degree in Physical Education. He was hired as a teacher and coach at the Ashtabula (Ohio) High School where he worked until his retirement. Early in his teaching career, Adam took two graduate courses at Youngstown State University but did not continue because his coaching, teaching, and family responsibilities demanded his full time.

In 1958, before he began his coaching career, Adam married Betty Miller whom he had met in Ashtabula. He and Betty have two grown children, RoLesia and Reginald or 'Rickey.'[17]

**Pat Montjoy** attended the University of California at Los Angeles (UCLA) and while there endorsed and promoted various products and services in television advertisements. She later moved to Chicago and became a legal secretary, working nights. That schedule, she said, enabled her 'to get some work done in a busy law firm.' In 2005, with my cousin Sandra Danforth, I spent an afternoon and evening with Pat in Chicago and found her to be energetic and friendly with a good sense of humor. Pat took us to a fine Italian restaurant on Michigan Avenue and told us several amusing stories about growing up in Southern Illinois and Charleston. Unfortunately, I have forgotten them all.[18]

Pat died from a series of strokes which, over a period of years, developed into Alzheimer's Disease. Her final, fatal stroke, came on September 9, 2019.

Because of memory loss and associated symptoms, she suffered a great deal before she died.

During her later years, she and her son, James "Jimmy" Booker, lived together and helped each other with their difficulties.[19]

**Jerome Price** shared some of his experiences with me since leaving Charleston. "I graduated from Charleston High School on a Friday and left for Camp Pendleton on Wednesday. I had it all set up before I graduated. Because I had graduated in 1956, before Johnny was murdered, I knew nothing about it until the following year. I was in a Marine Corps POX store in Japan when I noticed the May 1957 issue of *True Police Cases.* The lead article, 'Violent Skies over Sikeston' featured the murder of Johnny Malugen and the rape of his girlfriend."

"During my 13 months in Japan," Jerome said, "I learned to speak and understand Japanese easily. It sounds like English and is easy to pronounce. I didn't learn reading, writing, or grammar because I had no need for them. I got an excellent education in the Marine Corps."

After completing two years of active duty, Jerome moved to Chicago and drove City buses for 34 years and then drove Hertz and Greyhound buses for six more years. He said, "I enjoyed my work immensely and earned more money than many people with much more formal education than I had."

During my several conversations with Jerome, I found him to be upbeat, friendly, and articulate.

In 1959, Jerome married Eula Johnson from East St. Louis and adopted her two children from a previous marriage. During their 13-year marriage Eula gave birth to four children giving the couple a total of six. Eula died in 1972, after which Jerome married Pat Fowler. Pat gave birth to two children giving the couple a total of eight.

As of 2014, Jerome and Pat were living in Chicago and had been married for 42 years. They are Jehovah's Witnesses as was Jerome's first wife, Eula. Their faith has given them a strong source of meaning and direction for many years.[20]

As mentioned in Chapter 19, there is little information about **Joe Lester Slayton** after 1970, but records from the Social Security Administration indicate that he was still living as of 2010.[21]

**Lynn Twitty**, was Superintendent of the Sikeston, Missouri School System during the racial protests following the murder of Johnny Malugen.

In 1980, he became one of a four-man committee to achieve a closer and better cooperation between Southeast Missouri State University and school districts in the area. *Sikeston Standard Democrat, 1980.*[23]

## Endnotes

1. Dee Bonner, Interview by author, November 8, 2004

2. Mable Bradford Robinson, Interviews by author, March 18, 2014; April 21, 2014. Letter to author, July 1, 2014. Interviews by author, August 2014 & December 23, 2014

3. *Standard-Democrat*, August 15, 1997

4. Frank Nickell, Interview by author, July 8, 2010

5. *Standard-Democrat*, August 15, 1997

6. Frank Nickell, Interview by author, July 8, 2010

7. John Goodin, Interview by author, June 15, 2010

8. Adam Holman, Interview by author, 2015

9. Leatha Crenshaw Hale, Interviews by author, November 7, 2005, June 7, 2010, & October 13, 2014

10. Dr. Willie Curtis – Political Science Department – USNA *https://www.usna.edu/PoliSci/facultybio/curtis.ph - accessed December 23, 2018*

11. Gail Pang. Missouri University Extension, Mississippi County, Charleston, Missouri. Interview by author, December 2019

12. Terry Parker. McMikle Funeral Home, Charleston, Missouri. Interview by author, January 24, 2020

13. Lynn Wayne Hester's prison discharge note obtained by the author from the Missouri Department of Corrections, 2004.

14. Phone call by author to home of Lynn Wayne and Mary Hester, June 20, 2010

15. Phone call by author to the Edwards Funeral Home in Doniphan, Missouri, July 13, 2010

16. Phone call to Diane LaCroix, June 21, 2010

17. Adam Holman, Interview by author, March 18, 2014; Betty Holman, Interview by author, December 22, 2014

18. Patricia Montjoy, Interview by author, May 20, 2005

19. Mable Bradford Robinson, Interview by author, February 2020

20. Jerome Price, Interviews by author, March 6, 2014; March 18, 2014; May 16, 2014; September 25, 2014; December 22, 2014

21. Sharon Sanders. Librarian/historian for the Cape Girardeau, Missouri newspaper, *Southeast Missourian,* Interview by author, 2012

22. Lynn Twitty (1909-1997) Superintendent of Sikeston, Missouri Schools for 20 years. He was Sikeston's "Man of the Year" in 1963. *Southeast Missourian,* March 11, 1997

# 21

# Epilogue

To sum up my ideas on race: I believe that we should treat people of different ethnic, religious, economic, national, or political persuasions with respect. Before sharing more of my thoughts, I want to tell you something about the culture in which I grew up. I was born in the Missouri Bootheel in 1939 during the "Jim Crow" era and before the modern Civil Rights era began. When I was growing up, the social morals in the Bootheel were similar to those of the Deep South. Like any child would, I absorbed the beliefs and attitudes of the culture in which I grew up. However, as I grew older and was exposed to a wider experience and different influences, I began to look at my beliefs and attitudes from a different perspective.

Prejudice and discrimination can be based on almost anything that distinguishes one population or group from another. We tend to think that if people are different from us there must be something wrong with them, but as Dr. Arun Gandhi, explains:

An analysis of conflicts around the world today will readily reveal that they all have roots in the gross lack of respect people have for those with economic, religious, educational, nationalistic, or cultural differences.[1]

Those conflicts do not have to mean physically injuring or killing people. Prejudice and discrimination alone, over the long-term, can erode the physical and emotional health, and the economic stability of entire populations.

Our "saving grace" is that we can CHOOSE to respect people who are different from us. Despite our inclinations, we can decide to treat people better regardless of their racial or cultural heritage, the language they speak, or what part of town they come from. If we treat people with respect, they are more likely to respect us.

Most prejudices are learned at an early age from family, friends, and the broader culture.[2] When we are old enough to do our own thinking and have been exposed to a broader experience, we may find reason to take a stand against our own prejudices. They will not, however, disappear upon command. My personal experience is that shedding racial prejudice is like peeling an onion. After the first layer comes off, we eventually find another, and so on until we think it's gone.

Jane Cooper, now Stacy, was a close friend of Johnny Malugen and was a college freshman when she came to Johnny's funeral. She had no awareness of having racial prejudice, but after the funeral she became extremely angry at black people in general. Many years later she said, "I learned from that experience that we all have prejudice that we are not aware of and shouldn't consider ourselves immune to it."[3]

Deborah Betts Turner and another African American woman whose name I can't remember, told me that most black people in the area believed all along that a white person had committed the murder and rape. This belief was obviously not based on the testimony of June Castleberry, but, I believe, on black history. During slavery and the Jim Crow era, a white person could get away with blaming a black person for a crime he or she had committed. The black person had no means of defense because of the power and prejudice of the white majority.

This kind of scapegoating[4] has been known to occur today. Lynn Hester and Joe Slayton wore brown masks[5] and Slayton admitted to having imitated a "black accent" when threatening June Castleberry. This indicates that the two, or at least Slayton, consciously and deliberately intended to shift the blame for their crimes unto a black person (who did not exist). Given these circumstances, I doubt that June was lying about the race of her assailant, at least not consciously.

According to the *New Oxford American Dictionary*[6] a mob is "a large crowd of people, especially one that is disorderly and intent on causing trouble or violence." Most people would not do alone what they would in a mob. I believe the students who marched downtown in Charleston after the murder displayed *elements* of a mob mentality although nobody was physically injured and there was no property damage. The protest, as it was called, could have gotten out of hand had law enforcement officers not been present. Most of the *individuals* in this group were, in my opinion, decent people. I say this because I knew most of them. I firmly believe, however, that what the mob *itself* did was wrong. It was an affront to the African American citizens in our community and in our high school. That said, some of the marchers were probably responding to their hurt and grief as well as to their anger and prejudice. Paul Hill, for example, said, "We was just so hurt, we didn't know what to do."[7]

Although I disapproved of the way my black schoolmates were treated after the murder, it did not occur to me to speak out against it openly. If I had thought of it, I probably would not have spoken out because at that time I lacked the confidence and self-assurance to do so. Out of a student body of 350, not one person that I knew of spoke out openly although most would have discussed it in their own homes or with close friends.

Why didn't we speak out? I think our culture of prejudice and discrimination was the main reason but not the only one. I suspect that many of those who thought it was wrong, like myself, lacked the confidence and assurance to stand apart from their peers. Like most teenagers, we were very dependent on the approval and acceptance of our school mates, our peers. We were not yet sure "who we were."

Standing apart from those who give us acceptance and support can be frightening for anyone, even for the few who do it. Fear of rejection by our fellow humans takes its root in a realistic dread of abandonment. Those who do take this risk need strong convictions, confidence, and a good reason to do so. They also need courage which has less to do with feeling than with choice.

True racial harmony cannot develop until *both* races, white and black, rid themselves of prejudice to the extent that they can associate with one another on a friendly and equal basis. To begin this process, however, some individuals must be willing and able to step out with assurance and risk rejection by members of their own race. This can be frightening because of the fear of finding oneself in a "no man's land," between two warring factions with no source of support, guidance, or encouragement.

Attempts to promote peace between groups can also lead to great risks on the national and international scenes. Mohandas "Mahatma" Gandhi, Martin Luther King Jr., Anwar Sadat, and Yitzhak Rabin are just a few of those who have been assassinated because of their efforts to bring harmony between two warring groups. All of these leaders were killed by citizens of their own country.

Although not speaking out publicly, some of us white students supported our black schoolmates quietly by treating them with respect and acceptance. Jane Banta, for example, got to know Pat Montjoy well enough to call her twenty years after graduation and invite her to our twentieth high school class reunion. When the black students walked into the school for the first time, some of the white students, as well as their teachers, were standing there to greet them. When Jerome Price and Adam Holman were denied entrance to a restaurant on the way back from a track meet, a white boy on the team offered to "stand up" for them. When a crowd of white boys attempted to prevent four black students from entering the school on the Wednesday after the murder, some white senior boys assisted Mr. Williams in persuading the troublemakers to let the students in. Although none of the students at Charleston High School had openly defended their black schoolmates in 1957, three white boys - Everett Holley, Charles Ledbetter, and Charlie Babb - did risk rejection and ridicule when they stood up for six black students who had enrolled in the A. D. Simpson Junior High School in 1963. Steve Betts, one of the six, said that before the three white students stood up for them the black students were afraid to go to the rest room alone for fear of being attacked.

The three boys were socially skilled, physically strong, and of good *character.* Steve Betts said, "They got along with us black kids when we were being intimidated and treated us as equals."

Betts said, "It was not only their good character that made it possible for them to protect us; they were strong. All of them played football, and 'if you got hit, you knew you'd had been hit.' The strongest was Charlie Babb." Charlie played first string safety for the Miami Dolphins when they played in five Super Bowls and won the first two, 1972 and 1973.

Steve Betts said, "When we grew up Steve Ledbetter and I became good friends. One day he asked me if I would be willing to preach his funeral if I outlived him. I said I would."

An old issue that has become a "hot" issue in southern states during the last several years concerns the flying of the Confederate flag in public places. For African Americans this flag can symbolize a history of slavery, abuse, and hate. For white southerners with ancestors who fought for the Confederacy during the Civil War, or even died, the flag could mean respect for their forebears.

The NAACP has been, for some time, spearheading an aggressive campaign to outlaw the use of the Confederate flag in public places. As for back as 1993, Dr. Arun Gandhi wrote: "If the goal is to achieve true integration in the hearts of the people of the nation so that all can live with dignity and freedom, then aggressively fighting over a symbol is perhaps the wrong way to achieve it." The issue of the Confederate flag seems to have only grown more bitter. Now that the die has been cast, the NAACP will have to take the battle to a new level, and the escalation could go on until one side or the other is legally restrained, or too tired to continue the fight. Neither of these outcomes will be a lasting victory.[8]

A month after the racially motivated massacre of nine African Americans in a South Carolina AME church on June 17, 2015, the South Carolina Legislature voted to remove the Confederate flag from the grounds of its State House.[9] Four months later, the student senate at the University of Mississippi voted to remove the Mississippi state flag from their campus grounds because it included an image of the Confederate flag. The issue has been divisive and bitter across the entire state.[10] How these events will play out in the long run remains to be seen.

We all know that those who report and interpret the news, like anyone else, can be biased by their own beliefs and preconceptions. Another reason for lack of objective reporting is that the media do not exist in a vacuum. They are businesses in a competitive world and are under pressure to get the news out while it is still news. They may not have time to hear and understand the whole story whereas writers and editors of weekly or monthly publications have more time to study and understand the issues and facts. TV coverage, with its dramatic impact, can give the impression that our country is more polarized than it actually is. These visual images and interpretations can aggravate anger and prejudice on both sides.

I believe, however, that taken as a whole, the media in the United States do a reasonably good job *given the extreme degree of polarization we have today.* Despite biases there are also reasonable differences of opinion and points of view.

In 1983, my wife, Moreen, and I were on Ambergris Caye, an island off the coast of Belize. We were eating in a small restaurant where we were served by Suzannah, a tall, slender, black woman with whom we talked for quite a while. I felt that something was "in the air," something I had not experienced before. Later, upon reflection, I realized it was something that was *not* in the air, a level of comfort and enjoyment derived from an interpersonal experience in which race played absolutely no part.

On Ambergris Caye, a black woman named Moreen[11] would come up and take our toddler from my wife's arms and into hers without saying a word. That level of comfort was as if we were all in the same family. That was, at least in part, because there is only one family, the human family.

## Endnotes

1. Arun Ghandi, *Legacy of Love: My Education in the Path of Nonviolence,* Gandhi Worldwide Education Institute, Copyright 2003.

2. One exception to the learning of prejudice from one's family or culture is experiencing traumatic events in connection with a member or members of a different race, ethnic group, and other characteristic. This can easily occur in warfare, an example of which is post traumatic stress disorder.

3. Jane Cooper Stacy, Interview by author, July 21, 2010

4. Elwood Watson, "The Scapegoating of Black Men." March 27, 2017, a blog.

5. A caveat concerning the inference that Hester and Slayton wore brown masks to make it look like their crimes were committed by black people is that they planned to wear masks to rob *filling stations* with *no intention of murdering and raping.* Black masks worn during the commission of crimes are not unusual and don't have to mean that the perpetrators want to deceive witnesses into thinking the crimes were committed by African American people; they just don't want to get caught. In cowboy movies, stagecoach and train robbers almost always wore black masks, but there were almost no black people in these movies to blame it on. Whatever the intentions of Hester and Slayton were, the deception worked. In the author's mind the fact that Slayton, after raping June, faked a 'black accent' when telling her that he had to 'get to St. Louis fast' indicates that he was *deliberately* trying to blame their crimes on a black person or black persons.

6. *New Oxford American Dictionary*, Eds. Angus Stevenson & Christine A. Lindberg. Oxford University Press, 3rd Ed., August 2010.

7. Paul Hill, Interview by author, August 18, 2005

8. Ghandi, Arun, *Legacy of Love: My Education in the Path of Nonviolence,* Gandhi Worldwide Education Institute, Copyright 2003.

9. Charleston, SC church shooting. Wikipedia https://en.wikipedia.org/wiki/Charleston_church_shooting accessed 2018

10. Ole Miss students vote to remove state flag, and its Confederate-emblem PBS https://www.pbs.org//ole-miss-students-vote-remove-state-flag-Confederate-emblem - accessed February 20. 2019

11. Her name and my wife's name were spelled the same way. That's the way it is in families.

# 21.5

# 1958 Photos and Documents

Left to Right: Weber Gilmore, Arthur Bruce, Lynn Wayne Hester, & John Dennis, February 21, 1958, the day after Hester' arrest

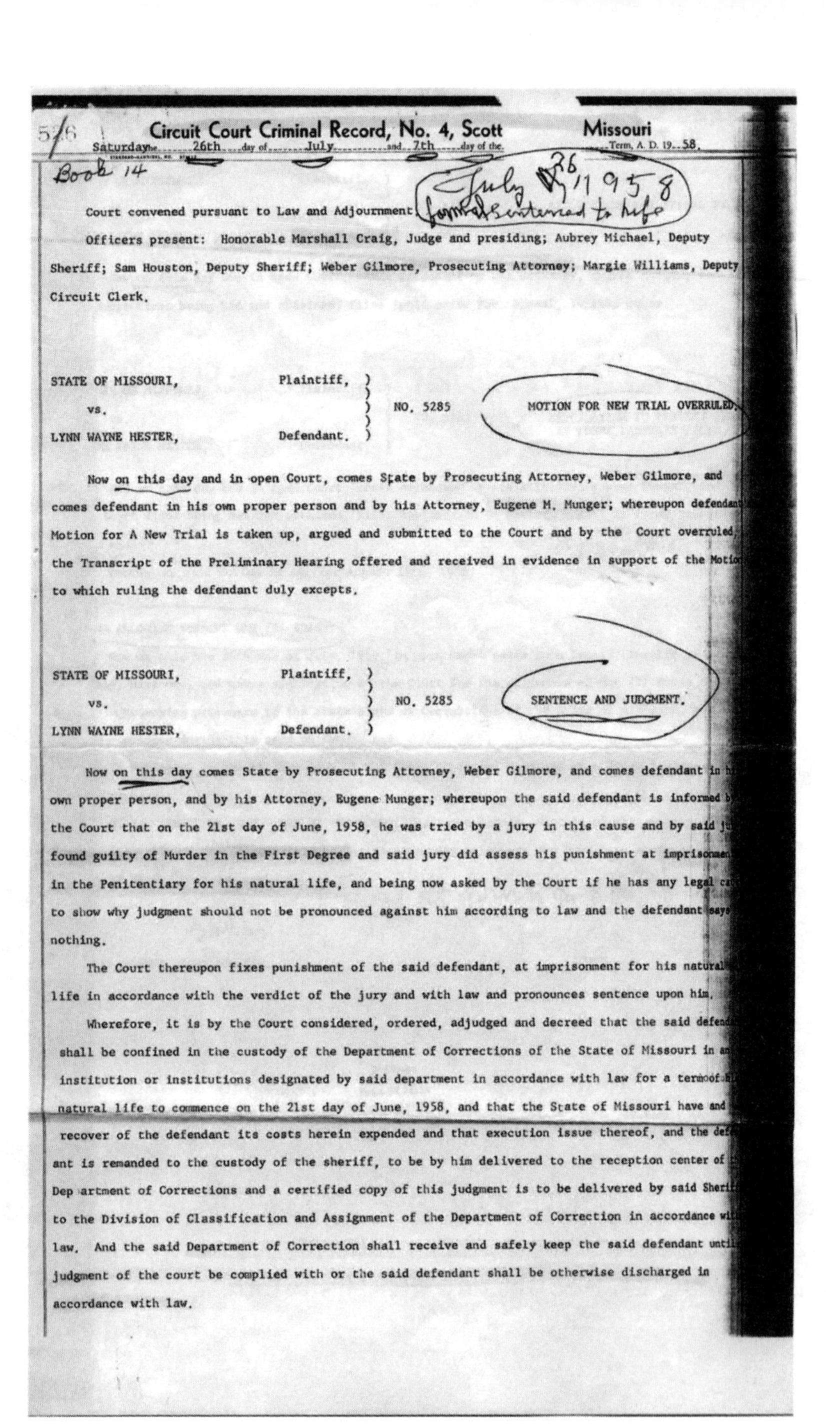

526 Circuit Court Criminal Record, No. 4, Scott Missouri
Saturday the 26th day of July and 7th day of the Term, A. D. 19 58.

Book 14

July 26, 1958
formal sentenced to life

Court convened pursuant to Law and Adjournment.

Officers present: Honorable Marshall Craig, Judge and presiding; Aubrey Michael, Deputy Sheriff; Sam Houston, Deputy Sheriff; Weber Gilmore, Prosecuting Attorney; Margie Williams, Deputy Circuit Clerk.

STATE OF MISSOURI, Plaintiff, )
vs. ) NO. 5285 MOTION FOR NEW TRIAL OVERRULED.
LYNN WAYNE HESTER, Defendant. )

Now on this day and in open Court, comes State by Prosecuting Attorney, Weber Gilmore, and comes defendant in his own proper person and by his Attorney, Eugene M. Munger; whereupon defendant's Motion for A New Trial is taken up, argued and submitted to the Court and by the Court overruled, the Transcript of the Preliminary Hearing offered and received in evidence in support of the Motion to which ruling the defendant duly excepts.

STATE OF MISSOURI, Plaintiff, )
vs. ) NO. 5285 SENTENCE AND JUDGMENT.
LYNN WAYNE HESTER, Defendant. )

Now on this day comes State by Prosecuting Attorney, Weber Gilmore, and comes defendant in his own proper person, and by his Attorney, Eugene Munger; whereupon the said defendant is informed by the Court that on the 21st day of June, 1958, he was tried by a jury in this cause and by said jury found guilty of Murder in the First Degree and said jury did assess his punishment at imprisonment in the Penitentiary for his natural life, and being now asked by the Court if he has any legal cause to show why judgment should not be pronounced against him according to law and the defendant says nothing.

The Court thereupon fixes punishment of the said defendant, at imprisonment for his natural life in accordance with the verdict of the jury and with law and pronounces sentence upon him.

Wherefore, it is by the Court considered, ordered, adjudged and decreed that the said defendant shall be confined in the custody of the Department of Corrections of the State of Missouri in an institution or institutions designated by said department in accordance with law for a term of his natural life to commence on the 21st day of June, 1958, and that the State of Missouri have and recover of the defendant its costs herein expended and that execution issue thereof, and the defendant is remanded to the custody of the sheriff, to be by him delivered to the reception center of the Department of Corrections and a certified copy of this judgment is to be delivered by said Sheriff to the Division of Classification and Assignment of the Department of Correction in accordance with law. And the said Department of Correction shall receive and safely keep the said defendant until judgment of the court be complied with or the said defendant shall be otherwise discharged in accordance with law.

Hester's Court Records 1958

Page 527
Book 14

| | | | |
|---|---|---|---|
| [ST]ATE OF MISSOURI, Plaintiff, | ) | | |
| vs. | ) | NO. 5285 | APPLICATION FOR APPEAL FILED. |
| [L]YNN WAYNE HESTER, Defendant. | ) | | |

Now on this day and in open Court, comes defendant by his Attorney, Eugene Munger, and leave [o]f Court first being had and obtained, files Application For Appeal, in this cause.

| | | | |
|---|---|---|---|
| [S]TATE OF MISSOURI, Plaintiff, | ) | | |
| vs. | ) | NO. 5285 | APPLICATION TO PERFECT APPEAL IN FORMA PAUPERIS FILED. |
| [L]YNN WAYNE HESTER, Defendant. | ) | | |

Now on this day and in open Court, comes defendant by his Attorney, Eugene Munger, and leave [o]f Court first being had and obtained, files Application To Perfect Appeal In Forma Pauperis, in [th]is cause.

appealed

Hearing on said Motion is set for August 14th, 1958.

[OR]DER ALLOWING SHERIFF ONE (I) GUARD:

Now on this the 26th day of July, 1958, in open Court comes John Dennis, Sheriff of Scott [Co]unty, Missouri, and makes application to the Court for the allowance of One (1) Guard to assist [hi]m in conveying prisoners to the State Board of Corrections of the State of Missouri, who have [b]een sentenced during this term of Court, and

IT APPEARING TO THE SATISFACTION OF THE COURT, That the services of a Guard is necessary for [th]is purpose,

IT IS, THEREFORE, THE ORDER OF THE COURT, That John Dennis, Sheriff of this County, be, and he [i]s hereby allowed One (1) Guard to assist in conveying prisoners who have been sentenced at this [te]rm of Court.

Hester received at prison on 8/22/58
selon

[I]T IS ORDERED COURT ADJOURN. JUDGE.

page 547
Book 14

Court convened pursuant to Law and Adjournment.

Officers present: Honorable Marshall Craig, Judge and presiding; John Dennis, Sheriff; Weber Gilmore, Prosecuting Attorney; Lloyd G. Briggs, Circuit Clerk. 6 Sept 1958

Pleaded guilty
Sentenced ~~reduced~~ to 15 years

STATE OF MISSOURI, Plaintiff, )
vs. ) NO. 5301 FORMAL ARRAIGNMENT PUNISHMENT FIXED.
JOSEPH LESTER SLAYTON, Defendant. )

Now on this day and in open Court, comes State by Prosecuting Attorney, Weber Gilmore, and come defendant in person in custody of the Sheriff and with his Attorneys, Harry C. Blanton and Roy F. Hough, heretofore appointed by the Court.

Whereupon the Court finds that the defendant has had an opportunity and reasonable time to consult with his said attorneys and with a friend; and defendant and his attorneys being present in open Court, defendant is formally arraigned and enters a plea of guilty to the charge in the Information; and the Court being fully advised of and concerning the premises doth fix the defendant's punishment at fifteen (15) years in an institution to be designated by the Department of Correction of the State of Missouri.

6 / Sept / 58
Pleaded guilty ~~statutory rape~~, sentenced 15 years

STATE OF MISSOURI, Plaintiff, )
vs. ) NO. 5301 SENTENCE AND JUDGMENT.
JOSEPH LESTER SLAYTON, Defendant. )

Upon an information charging the defendant with Statutory Rape.

Now on the .th day of September, 1958, comes the State of Missouri by the prosecuting Attorne and comes also the defendant in proper person in open court, and whereupon the court informed the defendant of his right to counsel and explained wherein the exercise of said right might be of benefit to the defendant and appoints Harry C. Blanton and Roy F. Hough, attorneys to act as couns for the defendant and notifies said counsel that a reasonable time will be allowed in which to pre pare the defense. Whereupon, after this defendant has had an opportunity and reasonable time to consult with his said counsel and with a friend and both defendant and his said counsel being pres in open court, defendant is duly arraigned and enters a plea of guilty to the charge of Statutory Rape, a felony, and the court states to the defendant that he has voluntarily entered his plea of guilty to the said charge, and now asks the defendant is he has any legal reason to give why judgment should not be pronounced upon him in accordance with his plea of guilty and the defendant says noti

And the court thereupon fixes the punishment of the defendant at imprisonment in an institut to be designated by the Department of Corrections of the State of Missouri in accordance with law for a term of Fifteen (15) years and pronounces sentence in accordance therewith.

WHEREFORE, it is by the court considered, ordered, adjudged and decreed that the said defend shall be confined in the custody of the Department of Corrections of the State of Missouri in a institution or institutions designated by said department in accordance with law for a period of Fifteen (15) years to commence on the 6th day of September, 1958, and that the State of Missouri have and recover of the defendant its costs herein expended and that execution issue thereof, an

Slayton's Court Records 1958

the defendant is remanded to the custody of the sheriff, to be by him delivered to the reception center of the Department of Correction and a certified copy of this judgment is to be delivered by said sheriff to the Division of Classification and Assignment of the Department of Correction in accordance with law. And the said Department of Correction shall receive and safely keep the said defendant until the judgment of the court herein be complied with or the said defendant shall be otherwise discharged in accordance with law.

ORDER ALLOWING SHERIFF ONE (I) GUARD:

Now on this the 6th day of September, 1958, in open/Court comes John Dennis, Sheriff of Scott County, Missouri and makes application to the Court for the allowance of one (1) Guard to assist him in conveying prisoners to State Department of Corrections of the State of Missouri, who have been sentenced during this term of Court, and

IT APPEARING TO THE SATISFACTION OF THE COURT, That the services of a Guard is necessary for this purpose,

IT IS, THEREFORE, THE ORDER OF THE COURT, That John Dennis, Sheriff of this County, be, and he is hereby, allowed one (1) Guard to assist in conveying prisoners who have been sentenced at this term of Court.

IT IS ORDERED COURT ADJOURN. JUDGE.

Name HESTER, Lynn Wayne | No. 74264-MJ | Inst. MSP | Race W | Sex M | 9-12T | Flat T. | Nat. L

Offense TC Murder 1st Degree

ELIGIBLE June, 1959 | Sentence Nat. Life | From 7-26-58 | County Scott

Received 8-22-58 | Term OF Court July, 1958 | Age & Conv. 18 | Prev. Conv. None

Birth Date 11-27-39 | Birthplace | Nativity Mo. | Religion Bapt | Ed. 9th

Height 5'11" | Weight 154 | Hair Brn | Eyes Blue | Complex. Ruddy | Phy. Char.

Occupation Mechanic | Marital Status | Children B G | Judge

Co-Defendants

7-17-70

Parole Action

| Date | Remarks | Date | Remarks |
|---|---|---|---|
| 9-12-59 | Hear Sept 1962 | 10-21-69 | Rev Oct 1970 |
| 9-4-62 | Rev Sept 1963 & Exam by Rock | 11-3-70 | Rev Oct 1971 |
| 9-3-63 | Rev Sept 1964 | 2-28-72 | Rev Oct 1972 |
| 9-4-64 | Rev Sept 1965 | Date RELEASED Hold - Orders - - Escapes - - Others | |
| 9-8-65 | Rev Sept 1966 | 10-11-72 | Hear Oct 1973 |
| 9-14-66 | Rev Sept 1967 | 9-27-73 | Long Range Parole Plng |
| 9-11-67 | Request Off Comm Report | | |

Hester's Prison Record 1974

Name SLAYTON, Joseph Lester | No. 74368-MJ | Inst. MSP | Race W | Sex M | 9-12T 8-11-71 ~~12-11-69~~ | Flat T. ~~9-11-70~~

Offense PG TC PG: Burglary 2nd & Stealing

ELIGIBLE July, 1959 | Sentence 3 yrs (3, Conc) | From 6-21-67 | County St. Louis

Received 5-12-69 | Term OF Court May 1967 | Age & Conv. 17 | Prev. Conv. one

Birth Date | Birthplace | Nativity Mo. | Religion | Ed.

Height | Weight | Hair | Eyes | Complex. | Phy. Char.

Occupation | Marital Status | Children B G | Judge

Co-Defendants no jail time

Parole Action

| Date | Remarks | Date | Remarks |
|---|---|---|---|
| 6-23-59 | Hear Sept 1960 | 11-4-58 | Escape from min |
| 9-8-60 | Rev. Sept. 1961 | 11-7-58 | RETURNED 6 mos |
| 9-18-61 | off & Comm | | |
| 11-6-61 | Exam by Rock; Rev Sept 1962 | Date | Hold RELEASED Others |
| 9-21-62 | Rev Sept 1963 | 12-2-65 | Home & Emp |
| 9-3-63 | Rev Sept 1964 | 8-30-67 | Returned JAN 18 1966 |
| 9-4-64 | Exam by Gukleman; Progress Report | 7-67 | Waived |
| 10-8-64 | Rev Sept 1965 | 8-8-67 | Revoked PAROLE |
| 9-8-65 | Recheck O&C | 8-11-67 | 1/2 (B.O.) |
| 11-19-65 | Progress Report | 4-30-68 | TRANSFERRED TO MSP |

MBPP-130

PAROLE ACTION

| DATE | REMARKS | DATE | REMARKS |
|---|---|---|---|

Slayton's Prison Record 1970

Mable Bradford Robinson (right) & Friend 2014

June Castleberry's Grave Marker 1997

# Historical Context: 1900-1950

# The Nation and the Bootheel[1] Charleston

During the early 1900s, racial prejudice and discrimination were by no means limited to the southern United States. An illustration of this maybe seen in the documentary film by Ken Burns, *Unforgivable Blackness*,[2] which shows the response to Jack Johnson's victory over the white James J. Jeffries in 1910 to become the first African American professional world heavyweight boxing champion: "The outcome of the fight triggered race riots that evening—the Fourth of July—all across the United States, from Texas and Colorado to New York and Washington, D.C. Johnson's victory over Jeffries had dashed white dreams of finding a "great white hope" to defeat the black Johnson. Many whites felt humiliated by the defeat of Jeffries." It has been estimated that between 11 and 26 people were killed in the riots and hundreds more injured when whites attacked blacks who were celebrating Johnson's victory.

* * *

## *Violence and Intimidation in the Bootheel*

During the first half of the 20th century, life for African Americans living in the Missouri Bootheel[2] was very difficult. In addition to discrimination by law and custom, there were at least three lynchings in Mississippi County, Missouri.[3,4]

### *Charleston, July 4, 1910*

Two Negroes who killed [a] white planter, [were] dragged from jail and hanged. [The] mob tried to burn darktown. These two men were Sam Fields and Robert Coleman.[3]

### *Charleston, 1924*

December 18, Charleston, Mo.: A mob of over 200 men overpowered the sheriff in his office in order to get possession of Roosevelt Grigsby, 20 years old, who was alleged to have attempted to attack a white girl. He was dragged across the courtyard and hanged from a tree within 50 feet of the sheriff's office. A bullet was fired through his body which was then cut down, tied to an automobile, and dragged through the streets of the Negro section.[4]

This account does not include the fact that after the noose was put around Grigsby's neck and his feet were off the ground, he held onto the rope to keep his neck from supporting his entire weight. A boy climbed the tree and shook the rope until Roosevelt had to let go. After his body was dragged to "colored town" it was *burned* there. My father, who was 17 at the time, told me about this lynching once, and only once. My father and grandfather witnessed this outrage through a window in my grandfather's law office across the street from the courthouse. Although my grandfather had prevented a lynching years before when he was Prosecuting Attorney, in 1924 he no longer had the authority or means to intercede.

*Sikeston: 1942*

Perhaps the best remembered and most explicitly documented lynching in the Bootheel occurred in Sikeston, Missouri on of January 25, 1942. About 1:30 a.m., Cleo Wright, a black man, reportedly broke into the home of a white woman, Grace Sturgeon, whose husband was on active duty in World War II. Wright slashed Grace across her abdomen causing massive internal injuries: she blocked his six-inch blade from cutting her throat, nearly losing three fingers on the hand that saved her life...[he sliced] her lower abdomen as easily as one could make a deep pin scratch. She 'burned like fire' as her intestines 'just unfolded and fell from her body'.

Sturgeon's sister-in-law, who was living with her, screamed and called the police. Neighbors appeared and the police arrived. One neighbor, Jesse Whittley, joined Officer Hess Perrigan in a police car to search for the assailant. Officer Roy Beck entered the house, called an ambulance, and accompanied Grace in an ambulance to the hospital.

Within half an hour, Officer Perrigan and Mr. Whittley saw Wright, hands in his pockets, walking across Malone Avenue, a little more than a mile from Grace Sturgeon's home. His pants were said to be bloodstained. Perrigan stopped the car, got out, and searched Wright, finding a 'long keen bladed knife.' Wright then began violently resisting arrest which forced Perrigan and Whittley to wrestle him into the back seat of the police car. Perrigan, with his pistol drawn, got in the back seat beside Wright, and Whittley went to the front seat and began driving them to the jail. At that point Wright pulled out another knife he had hidden on his person and stabbed Perrigan in the mouth cutting the artery under his tongue. The injured officer fired his pistol ending the attack. Whittley then changed directions and drove to the hospital instead of the jail. Because of rapid arterial bleeding, Perrigan was taken immediately into emergency surgery, operated on, and survived.

Mrs. Sturgeon, whose abdomen had been slashed with a knife, had already arrived at the hospital. Emergency surgery had been performed and she survived as well.

As soon as Whittley delivered Officer Perrigan to the hospital, he was joined by Officer Beck, who had earlier accompanied Grace Sturgeon in the ambulance to the hospital. Beck got into the police car and took charge of Wright while Whittley drove to the jail. There Wright's gunshot wounds were examined for the first time. He had been shot four times with Perrigan's .45 caliber pistol, twice through the midsection, once through the right chest, and once through the right arm. Wright was immediately driven by ambulance to the hospital where he was treated surgically. Because blacks were given emergency treatment only and were not admitted to the hospital, Wright was then taken to his home. He was later visited by three police officers who stated that they thought he was dying. His family feared for his safety, and at the pleading of his wife and in-laws, the officers returned him to the jail and put him on a cot. He did not, however, receive any further medical attention.

During the night, word of the stabbing spread, and by morning a mob had formed. Just after 11: 30 a.m., Scott County Prosecuting Attorney David Blanton arrived and spoke to the crowd in an attempt to dissuade them from violence. The mob, however, rushed past the law enforcement officers, broke down the door into the room where Wright was on the cot, and dragged him down the hallway and into the street. There, they tied him by his legs to the rear bumper of a car and dragged him to the Sunset Addition where they burned his body. Whether he was dead when he was set on fire is a matter of conjecture.

The lynching received a great deal of attention in both the state and national media, but despite the efforts of David Blanton, the United States Attorney General Francis Biddle, and other law enforcement officials, not a single member of the lynch mob was convicted of a crime. Cleo Wright was the last person lynched in the Missouri Bootheel and in fact, the entire state of Missouri.[5]

This account is not meant to imply that Cleo Wright was not guilty of a heinous crime. A jury, even one including black members, may very well have imposed the death penalty. In any case, however, Wright was denied due process of law which is guaranteed by the Constitution, and a mob acted as judge, jury, and executioner.

*Just Across the River: 1909*

Cairo, Illinois is just across the Mississippi River from the Missouri Bootheel and 14 miles east of Charleston. In 1909, Cairo residents lynched a black man named Will James, accused of murdering a 7-year-old girl. After James was hanged, his body was riddled with bullets, dragged a mile on a rope, and burned before a crowd of ten thousand people. Burning the body of a lynched black man was not uncommon in those days. The body of a white man lynched the same evening was neither burned nor mutilated. Photographs were taken of Will James' lynching and made into picture post cards, one of which was titled, *"Half-Burned Head of James on a pole."*[6]

*Intimidation*

There were forms of intimidation by mobs less dramatic than lynchings but nevertheless effective. During World War II there was a shortage of farm workers in Butler County, Missouri because so many men were overseas fighting the war. An incident related to this shortage is summarized below:

In 1944, a mob of some 200 persons forced a Butler County farmer to remove from the county a Negro couple he had hired to help work the farm. The sheriff advised the farmer, Louis Cooper, that he was within his rights in hiring blacks, but it would be impossible to guarantee the safety of the couple.[7]

* * *

*The 1939 Sharecroppers' Demonstration*

Of historical interest but not involving violence or murder was the 1939 Sharecroppers Demonstration. This protest began after wealthy landowners in the Missouri Bootheel, to their financial advantage, evicted sharecroppers from their shacks in January 1939 in the middle of winter. To protest their eviction the sharecroppers, both black and white, lined highways 60 and 61 from Sikeston in Scott County to Hayti in Pemiscot County, a distance of 55 miles. The strikers had assembled temporary, makeshift shelters along the highways for their families. After five days, officials began removing the protesters in trucks provided by the State Highway Department and after two days had removed 1,300 of them. Many were unable to return to their former homes because their landlords refused to take them back. They went to various temporary encampments.[8]

Lorenzo Greene, a history professor at Lincoln University in Jefferson City, Missouri, visited these encampments and wrote:

"Hundreds of sharecroppers with their pitiable belongings congregated in groups. Men, women, young and old, boys and girls shivering in the cold, little children and even babies crying because of hunger, their swollen bellies indicative of lack of sufficient food. I saw their makeshift dwellings of wood, burlap, tin, cardboard, anything to protect them from the frigid weather. I saw them trying to cook over open fires, on makeshift stoves, or just standing about trying to keep warm."[9]

One of those children mentioned in the above paragraph was a toddler named Adam Holman who would graduate from Charleston High School in 1956 and go on to become a high school football and track coach in Ashtabula, Ohio.

Thad Snow was an outspoken landowner who knew the organizers of the strike and actively supported it. This made him very unpopular in the area, especially among other landowners. According to Fannie Cook, a novelist who visited the area, some white people, doctors, housewives, and cafe owners, were supportive of the strikers. She wrote, "Thad Snow is by no means the only planter who feels as he does, but others are afraid to speak out."[10]

* * *

*Everyday Life: Jim Crow*

The most pervasive forms of injustice in the Bootheel during this era were woven into the fabric of everyday life. The array of written and unwritten rules covered broad areas of life. White attitudes toward blacks continually eroded black confidence and self-esteem.

Racial discrimination, of course, included not only inferior schools but also segregated restaurants, movies, public bathroom facilities, and drinking fountains. Housing discrimination and extreme poverty resulted in many blacks living in shacks without running water or adequate heat. This is not to say that some white people did not live in poverty as well, especially during the Great Depression, but for most black people it was the norm with little hope of improvement. Job discrimination denied blacks the opportunity to exercise the skills they had and seldom allowed them to develop their natural abilities beyond those required for menial labor.

The forms and subtleties of discrimination and prejudice were so numerous and sometimes contradictory they cannot be easily explained or summarized. Describing racial relations in Sikeston during the 1940s, Dominic Capeci wrote, "Although blacks puzzled over being denied the use of restrooms in the Malone Theater but permitted to share those across the street at the Frisco Train Depot with white travelers, they understood the 'invisible line' that no one of either race dared cross no matter how inconsistent it seemed."[11]

According to racial mores, black people were expected to show an undue respect for the white majority and to "stay in their place." Those who failed to do so were often called "uppity" and could face serious consequences. This was especially true if a black man was seen as being too familiar with a white woman.

*"Miss Alfreda" Remembers*

Despite their prejudice against African Americans in general, it was common for whites to have good relationships with individual blacks, especially with those who worked for them. In 2004, I interviewed Alfreda Rogers, a ninety one-year-old woman living in

Charleston. She said, "I came here from Mississippi with my parents in 1924 when I was twelve years old. We were sharecroppers and lived on a series of farms: Perry Crenshaw's farm, the Babbs, the Moores, and several others. The people who owned the farms we lived on protected us from being beaten up when we had to go to East Prairie for firewood or through Bertrand. Blacks mostly lived near white farmhouses for protection. There were some bomb threats. I heard about the lynching of Roosevelt Grigsby in 1924 and the lynching in Sikeston in 1942, but I didn't see nothing of either one. After the lynching in Sikeston, when they drug the man behind a car. My father told me I'd better stay in the house and be careful. In times of danger, the white farmers would make sure their black sharecroppers were near their houses." Alfreda recalled the racial problems following the Malugen murder. She said, "I remember when Charleston High School was integrated in 1955. When the trouble happened after the murder, though, I lived in the country and didn't see any of it and never saw the patrol cars around the high school. Hattie May Kimball's brother was the bus driver, and it was his job to drive the black students to the high school. He was afraid and dropped them off several blocks from the school, but the people in charge told him to drive them all the way, and he did."[12]

*White Child, Black Child*

As illustrated by these examples of intimidation, discrimination, and violence, black people during the first half of the 20th century in the Missouri Bootheel faced difficult circumstances. Most white people, including myself, accepted the social system as normal because we had never known any other. As a child I knew very little about the extent or impact of discriminatory practices imposed on black people, and I suspect few other young white children did either. African American children, however, began to learn about these facts at an earlier age.

### *Hope*

As difficult and dangerous as life had been for black people during the first part of the 20th century, some progress in race relations did occur during that period. On a national level, according to the *Harvard Encyclopedia of American Ethnic Groups,*[13] black people became more visible in the arts, sciences, and in business, and there were more black lawyers, doctors, and educators. The armed forces were integrated in 1948 after blacks had fought alongside whites in both World War I and World War II. After 1937, Supreme Court decisions became more friendly to blacks and culminated in the 1954 landmark decision that "separate but equal schools" were unconstitutional.[14] The implementation of school desegregation, however, was left to the remaining decades of the century.

## Endnotes

1. The term "Missouri Bootheel" has been used to designate anywhere from three to eight counties in the extreme southeastern part of the state. In this book I use the term to include seven counties: Scott, Mississippi, New Madrid, Pemiscot, Dunklin, Stoddard, and Butler. Except for one incident in Butler County, the events recorded this book are confined to Mississippi and Scott Counties. Before the

area was drained of excessive water by the Little River Drainage District, the Bootheel area was sometimes called "Swampeast Missouri." Technically the area is referred to as the "Southeastern Lowlands."

2. *Ward, Geoffrey C. Unforgivable Blackness: The Rise and Fall of Jack Johnson* by Geoffrey C. Ward, Knoph Doubleday, August 4, 2010. ISBN 9780375710049

3. July 4, 1910 *Herald Democrat,* (a Los Angeles newspaper)

4. *Delta Dunklin Democrat,* December 1924, Kennett, Missouri

5. Capeci, Dominic J. Jr. *The Lynching of Cleo Wright,* The University Press of Kentucky, 1988

6. Cairo-Walking in Place - accessed January 9, 2011 www.walkinginplace.org/place There are several entries for this URL. Look for *"Cairo-Walking in Place"*

7. The author was first told of these events by Dr. Frank Nickell on March 7, 2009. I found this quote on Google via http://www.duboislc.org/MissouriBlacks/p07_CivilRights.html on April 26, 2010, but on January 15, 2019, this URL did not lead to the same information.

8. Stepenoff, Bonnie. *Thad Snow: A Life of Social Reform in the Missouri Bootheel..* University of Missouri Press, 2003, pp. 80, 83, 91-98, 135, 157-159

9. Greene, Lorenzo J. "Lincoln University's Involvement with the Sharecropper Demonstration in Southeast Missouri, 1939-1940" *Missouri Historical Review* 82 (October 1987): 24-50.

10. Stepenoff, Bonnie. *Thad Snow: A Life of Social Reform in the Missouri Bootheel.*. University of Missouri Press, 2003, pp. 80, 83, 91-98, 135, 157-159

11. Capeci, Dominic J. Jr. *The Lynching of Cleo Wright*, The University Press of Kentucky, 1988

12.. Alfreda Rogers, Interview by author, April 9, 2004

13. Themstrom, Stephan; Oriole, Ann; & Handlin, Oscar. *Harvard Encyclopedia of American Ethnic Groups.* Belknap Press of Harvard University, 1980

14. Brown vs Board of Education - https://en.wikipedia.org/wiki/Brown_v._Board_of_Education -accessed December 11, 2014

# Historical Context: 1950-2000 Charleston

Not only Charleston, Missouri but the whole country began a new era in race relations in the schools in 1954 following the Supreme Court ruling that "separate but equal schools" were unconstitutional. Sixteen months after the decision in Washington, eight black students voluntarily enrolled in Charleston High School. On the surface, for the most part, things appeared relatively quiet and uneventful, but the stage was set for a conflagration. The murder of Johnny Malugen and the rape of June Castleberry provided the match that lit the fire. The trouble following Johnny's murder may not have occurred in a different context.

In the current context, the words "segregation," "desegregation," and "integration" must be used differently. Desegregation is the elimination of segregation, the forced separation of black and white students. Integration means the unforced and harmonious coming together of black and white students on an equal basis. This can only be achieved by the students themselves and cannot be legislated.

A fourth term is "consolidation," the *forcing* of black and white students together whether they want to be or not. In Charleston, this has caused almost as much conflict as desegregation has, perhaps more.

The desegregation and consolidation of the junior high and elementary schools in Charleston occurred during the 1960s. Having begun at the high school level in 1955, the desegregation process moved through the lower grades and was completed in 1968.[1] During the desegregation phase, black parents were given the choice of sending their children to the segregated Lincoln School or one of the desegregated schools: the A. D. Simpson Junior High School, the Mark Twain Elementary School or the Eugene Field Elementary School. At the beginning of the *consolidation* phase, the Lincoln School was closed, and the students, both black and white, attended the same schools. Today that is the status of the entire school system.

One black student, Charlie Clark Jr., shared his experiences in the newly desegregated and then consolidated Mark Twain School. He was one of the few black students whose parents chose to enroll their children there. Charlie got along fairly well during the desegregated phase, although some of the black students gave him the cold shoulder, perhaps because he got along well with the white students. At one time the Clark family had lived in the country near a white family with children about Charlie's age, and they played together. This may have influenced Charlie's relationship with the white students.

When Charlie began the seventh grade, the Mark Twain School had been consolidated. Charlie said, "It came as a total shock to me. All hell broke loose, and I wished I was in a segregated school!

I got along fine with the white students but not the black students. They called me Honky Lover, Uncle Tom, or Oreo. Oreo meant black on the outside and white on the inside."[2] Carolyn and Nancy Bristo, both excellent African American students, also received sarcastic remarks because they got along with the white students.[3]

Charlie said he got along better with the black students at Charleston High School than he had at the Mark Twain School. The black and white students, he said, got along fairly well on the surface, but there was an undercurrent of tension, and any minor incident could cause a flare-up.[4] Charlie graduated from Charleston High School in 1974.

Linda Moxley, now Raines, a white student from Wyatt, graduated from Charleston High School in 1985. As a college student in 1988, she wrote a term paper for a history class titled, *"The Integration of Charleston Public Schools: Was it a Step Forward or Backward for the Relationship Between Blacks and Whites?"* Linda interviewed two Charleston High School Teachers and a former student who graduated the 1957, the year Johnny Malugen was killed. Based on these interviews and her own recollections as a student, Linda concluded that "the school was virtually unchanged during the thirty years since the integration program was introduced."

Regarding the Malugen murder, Linda wrote, "In a small town that still bore an extreme amount of prejudice, the scars would run deep and last for many years afterward."[5] Charlie Clark said, "There is still a lot of anger in the black community about these events. Blacks will talk about them among themselves but rarely with whites."[6]

Marshall Currin, President of the Mississippi County chapter of the National Association for the Advancement of Colored People (NAACP) and his wife, Helen, began teaching nonviolent methods of protest in the black community during the 1950s and 1960s. When Marshall died, Helen succeeded him as president of the NAACP chapter and continued his work. The Currins coordinated marches to protest segregation at the McCutchen Theater, the bus station, and restaurants. The marches received some outside help from other states and other NAACP chapters. A local white minister, Rev. Robert Burke, would meet the protesters downtown and pray with them but did not march with them.[7] Burke participated in civil rights activities such as Freedom Rides, in the deep South.[8]

Deborah Turner said there was another group of black protest marchers in Charleston that believed that violence was justified if the protesters were attacked. This group marched near, but not with, the nonviolent protesters.[9]

Marshall and Helen Currin owned the Creole Cafe, a black restaurant in Charleston, popularly known as the Currin Cafe. During one of the protest marches, the cafe caught fire, but the blaze was extinguished in time to save the building. The evidence indicated that the cause of the fire was arson committed with a rag doused with gasoline.[10] Helen Currin's niece, Gail Pang, said there were several other attempts to burn down the Cafe.[11]

Along with movie theaters, buses, and restrooms. all Charleston eating establishments in 1963 were segregated. One of these was Ellis' Confectionary, a popular ice cream parlor and soda fountain that also sold sandwiches. High school students liked to congregate there during the lunch hour, and farmers, businessmen, and retired people gathered to socialize over morning coffee. Blacks were allowed to order food to take out at Ellis' but could not go in and sit down.

In 1963, when Leora Easton, now Hamilton, was an eighth grader at the Lincoln School, she participated in a march to protest segregation at Ellis' "The march," she said, "began at the Currin Cafe at the intersection of Marshall and Elm Streets. There were quite a number of students and adults from various black churches." She said, "We lined up, side by side, holding hands, and singing 'We shall overcome.' A white man walked up and down in front of us like a military officer. He'd come up, stare into our faces, and spit on some of us. I think he was trying to intimidate us, but Mrs. Currin told us not to break the chain. We held calm and marched to Ellis' but were not allowed to go inside. Some of the protesters were arrested and jailed."[12]

The most volatile and dangerous racial situation in the area during the 1960s and early 1970s was in Cairo, Illinois. A few black activists from Cairo attempted to get involved with civil rights leaders in Charleston, but Helen Currin and Mississippi County Sheriff "Pedro" Simmons told them that Charleston could handle its own racial problems without their assistance. They did not of approve the tactics used by the civil rights leaders in Cairo during those troubled times.[13]

Helen Currin and Sheriff Simmons played pivotal roles in keeping anger from spilling over into violence in Charleston. They worked together consistently and successfully for many years to preserve and protect the social integrity of Charleston as it was affected by racial issues.[14]

A particularly violent year in American racial history was 1967 which included rioting, burning, and looting in major cities such as Cleveland, Detroit, and Newark. In late August of that turbulent year, Roy Wilkins, President of the NAACP, came to the little town of Charleston, Missouri and gave an address urging moderation in the African American struggle for respect and equal opportunity. Sheriff Simmons drove to Paducah, Kentucky and personally escorted Mr. Wilkins over the bridge spanning the Ohio River into Illinois, past Cairo, and then across the Mississippi River bridge into Missouri.[15] The local newspaper, *Enterprise-Courier,* urged all citizens, both black and white, to welcome Mr. Wilkins and listen to him carefully.

In a forceful and articulate speech, before 1,100 black and white citizens, Mr. Wilkins urged African Americans to "Push but don't riot, register to vote, get to know the leaders in your community, develop your own leadership, and avoid outside agitators who only want stir up trouble."[16]

Racial tension decreased in Charleston after the 1960s and 1970s but did not disappear. The October 27, 1994 issue of the *Enterprise-Courier* reported the following incident:

Racial tension in Charleston came close to erupting into a riot last Sunday afternoon when an angry group of 75 to 150 black residents marched on City Hall demanding answers to questions concerning an apparent suicide early Sunday morning of Elmer L. 'Elmo' Johnson in the county jail.

But the riot did not occur. A major crisis was averted by the intervention and mediation on the part of black leaders coupled with the cooperation of city officials and police and the willingness of people to listen. At the height of the tension Sunday, individuals in one part of the crowd leaving the City Hall to return to the Lincoln School for a discussion with leaders, bashed in four windows and pelted vehicles with bottles and/or rocks, and damaging at least five vehicles. Shots were fired in the direction of officers about this time and officers fired into the air. Another account of these events may be seen in the *St Louis Post-Dispatch on* October 3, 1994.

In spite of all this trouble, the most important fact was that there was enough trust and good will between African Americans and white leaders of the town to prevent the anger, rage, and distrust from escalating further.

Despite misunderstandings and conflict, the lives of African Americans in Charleston have improved since Johnny Malugen was killed in 1957. This is evident to anyone who lived in Charleston before that time and especially for those who had left town and come back years later. One example of progress occurred in 1972 when Charles Williams, a City Council member, was elected the first black mayor of Charleston. That would have been unlikely, if not impossible, in 1957.

Instead of living in small, poorly heated shacks with no running water or indoor toilets, almost all African Americans enjoy these amenities today. Gail Pang told me that blacks can live anywhere in Charleston they want if they have the money to buy a house. In spite of the drastic loss of jobs resulting from the mechanization of farming and loss of manufacturing in Charleston, there are some jobs in the area that black people can drive to.[17]

Before school desegregation began, there were no African American teachers in the Charleston School System except for the segregated Lincoln School. Since that time some black teachers and administrators have been highly respected by both black and white students.

Elder Steve Betts is the pastor of the Opportunity Church of God in Christ in Charleston and has been a Civil Rights activist there for many years. He was a prime mover in the founding of the Opportunity Outreach Center in Charleston which serves the African American community. During an interview by the author in 2009, he expressed his faith that whites and blacks could achieve mutual respect, learn to appreciate each other's points of view, and achieve more peaceful relationships. He said, "If I come to the table with preconceived notions – if I draw a line in the sand – I might as well not come. What we need is balance. We can't back down, but we have to avoid being provocative. This is not a problem that can't be solved."

There has been some racial mixing among the ministers in Charleston. Elder Betts said the Ministerial Alliance in Charleston includes both black and white ministers, and they have worked together on community projects. He said one black church in Charleston, the Shining Light Baptist Church, has a white minister from the area. Betts believes that if black and white ministers traded pulpits occasionally, it would improve interracial understanding, and it would help if the history of different forms of worship were explained.[18]

A positive long-term view was offered by ninety-one-year-old Alfreda Rogers who came to Charleston in 1924 from Mississippi at the age of twelve. She said she had seen a great deal of progress during her 80 years in Mississippi County and was optimistic about the future. "Things are better now. There has been some integration of housing in the poorer neighborhoods on the east side of Main Street. The cemetery was integrated by Reverend Steve Betts when his mother was buried. They dug a grave in the back of the cemetery because they thought that's what he wanted, but he got her buried up front. Back in 1955 and 1956 we had to go to the back door of a white house, but now we can go to the front door."[19]

An equally upbeat perspective comes from Rosemary Clark, born in 1937 in Armorel, Arkansas, a tiny community on a cotton plantation in the northeast corner of the state. Her mother brought her to Missouri when she was four years old, and she has lived in Charleston or nearby ever since. At 16 she married Charlie Clark, Sr., raised nine boys, and has worked her entire life, either on farms or in white people's houses.

Rosemary takes a humorous and down-to-earth view of the ideas and attitudes that white and black people have about each other. She said, "One thing I could never understand. That's why some white people thought blacks were dirty but would let them cook their food and take care of their kids. I wouldn't want a dirty person taking care of my kids and cooking my food. If they thought we were dirty, how'd they know we wouldn't slip some poison or something in their food?"

She continued: "Some black folks teach their kids not to like whites, and some white folks teach their kids not to like blacks. I wasn't raised to hate whites, and Charlie and I didn't raise our boys to hate whites. When Corey was young, he had a lot of white friends, and they'd spend the night with us, a whole bunch of them on the floor. We had to step over them. One of my black friends said something about 'rich, white, little Corey.' I said, 'He don't look white to me, and he shore ain't rich. She was an older lady.'"

Rosemary said, "I always got along with the white people I worked and cleaned for, and I put up with their funny habits. Black folks have just as many funny habits as whites. I don't care whether a person is black or white; it's how they do. Some blacks I don't want nothin' to do with, and some whites are the same. Some whites don't hate blacks; they just don't think they should marry."[20]

Rosemary creates comfortable relationships with almost everyone she knows, regardless of race."

When the author visits Charleston, some sixty years after the Malugen murder, he sometimes sees blacks and whites in restaurants and other public places engaging in spontaneous conversations. A complete social integration, meaning harmonious and unforced relationships between blacks and whites in all areas of life, however, is still a distant goal, but distant does not mean never. With most legal discrimination barriers removed, respect and trust among Charleston's residents of different colors can develop in their own time.

## Endnotes

1. Annette Robertson. Interview by author, January 24, 2011

2. Charlie Clark Jr. Interview by author, April 7, 2009

3. Mable Benson Mullins, Interview by author, December 30, 2009

4. Charlie Clark Jr. Interview by author, May 28, 2000

5. Linda Moxley Raines. *The Integration of Charleston Public Schools: Was it a Step Forward or Backward for the Relationship Between Blacks and Whites?* Unpublished college seminar paper, 1988.

6. Charlie Clark Jr, 2000

7. Deborah Betts Turner. Interview by author, August 22, 1997

8. Karen Giltz Moore. Interview by author, 2007

9. Deborah Betts Turner. Interview by author, 2014

10. Deborah Betts Turner, *Ibid,*

11. Gail Pang. Interview by author, February 7, 2015

12. Leora Easton Hamilton. March 17, 2011, summarized from a written account by Leora Hamilton

13. Gail Pang, Interview by author, April 17, 2015

14. Gail Pang, Interview by author, February 7, 2007; Alfreda Rogers, Interview by author, April 9, 2004; Deborah Betts Turner, Interview by author, August 22, 2005; Elder Steve Betts. Interview by author, November 24, 2009; and Ida McTigue Hurley, Interview by author, December 30, 2011, *and others*!

15. Gail Pang, Interview by author, 2015

16. *Enterprise-Courier,* August 3, 1967

17. Gail Pang, Interview by author, October 15, 2015

18. Elder Steve Betts, Interview by author, November 24, 2009

19. Alfreda Rogers, Interview by author, April 9, 2004

20. Rosemary Clark, Interview by author, 2006

# Annotated Bibliography

Branch, Taylor. *Martin Luther King Jr. and the Civil Rights Movement,* contained in *The American Story: Conversations with Master Historians.* Edited by David M. Rubenstein. Copyright 2019, Simon & Schuster.

This exciting account of the American Civil Rights Movement, focusing on Martin Luther King, Jr., reveals the astounding complexity of the politics and the diversity of conflicting means to a common goal. King not only had to fight those individuals and organizations bent on maintaining the status quo but also the leaders of groups opposing King's tactics and core beliefs.

Burnett, Mildred Reeves. *Charleston Had It All,* Acclaim Press, Morley, Mo., 2013. ISBN 13: 978-1-938905-49-0

The author provides a history of Charleston, Missouri based on her memories, the memories of others, old newspapers, and library sources. She gives us a feeling of what Charleston was like in bygone days. Her writing is casual, folksy, and easy to read as she tells about people, families, businesses, politics, agriculture, civil war history, floods caused by the Mississippi and Ohio Rivers, watermelon festivals, and "bingo trials."

Capeci, Dominic J. Jr. *The Lynching of Cleo Wright.* The University Press of Kentucky, 1988. ISBN 0-8131-2048-9

This book is a detailed account and analysis of the 1942 lynching of a black man in Sikeston, Missouri. The lynching received coverage from both state and national presses and provoked controversy and soul searching from Missouri all the way to the Congressional and Executive branches of the federal government. This was the last of 58 lynchings of black people that occurred in Missouri since 1889. During the same period 27 white people were lynched.

Douglass, Frederick. *Narrative of the Life of Frederick Douglass, an American Slave.* First published in 1845 by the Anti-Slavery Office, and later published in 2003 by Barnes and Noble Books. Copyright 2003. ISBN 978-1-59308-041-9

The following two quotes from Frederick Douglass can summarize a great deal of what this book is about:

"You have seen how a man was made a slave; you shall see how a slave was made a man."

*and*

"I have sometimes thought that a mere hearing of those songs [of the slaves] would do more to impress some minds with the horrible character of slavery than the reading of whole volumes of philosophy on the subject could do. To those songs I trace my first glimmering conception of the dehumanizing character of slavery. I can never get rid of that conception. Those songs will follow me, to deepen my hatred of slavery, and quicken my sympathies for my brethren in bonds."

In 1864, Douglass was called to the White House by Abraham Lincoln to discuss strategies for emancipation. Douglass was later given political appointments by presidents Grant (1871), Hayes (1877), Garfield (1881), and Benjamin Harrison (1891).

Franklin, John Hope & Higginbotham, Evelyn Brooks. *From Slavery to Freedom: A History of Negro Americans,* 9th edition. ISBN-13: 9780077407513

This classic panoramic history of the black race tells a story beginning with the dawn of civilization in Africa. The authors tell of millennia of migrations during which Negroes played pivotal roles in the development of several African countries and later in the Americas. It informs us of the struggles of black people to gain respect, freedom, and opportunity after they arrived in the New World. This book is equally suited for personal use or as a textbook. It is the latest edition of John Hope Franklin's classic history, revised and updated by Evelyn Brooks Higginbotham, Copyright 2010.

Gandhi, Arun, *Legacy of Love: My Education in the Path of Nonviolence.* Gandhi Worldwide Education Institute, Copyright 2003 ISBN 978-0-9823919-0-7

This is a memoir written by the grandson of Mohandas "Mahatma" Gandhi about his learning the principles and practices of nonviolence from his grandfather. Before going to India at age 12, Arun Gandhi had lived in apartheid South Africa where he suffered a great deal of prejudice, discrimination and humiliation. During his time in India he learned new ways to deal with and think about these experiences. This book contains many stories and anecdotes about his experiences with his father and grandfather, "Mahatma" Gandhi.

Greene, Lorenzo J., Kremer, Gary R., Holland, Antonio F. *Missouri's Black Heritage.* Columbia, Missouri: University of Missouri Press, 1993 ISBN 0-8262-0905-X

"This book describes in detail the struggles faced by many African Americans in their efforts to achieve full civil and political rights against the greatest odds." The authors tell us how slavery came to Missouri, what the life of a slave was like, and ways in which they adapted to it or resisted. The writers describe the African American experience during the Civil War, Reconstruction, World War I, the Great Depression, World War II, and the modern Civil Rights movement. The last chapter discusses the racial situation in Missouri during the 1980s and future prospects.

*Lynching: State by State & Race, 1882-1968*. University of Missouri-Kansas City School of Law.

This is a table of the 4,743 lynchings that occurred in the United States between 1882 and 1968 categorized by the state in which they occurred, how many there were, and whether they were black or white. States with the most lynchings were Mississippi (581), Georgia (531), Texas (493), Louisiana (391), and Alabama (347). There were no lynchings in Alaska, Hawaii, New Hampshire or Rhode Island. On average, except for Texas, there were more white people than black lynched in the western states.

McLachlan, Sean. *Missouri: An Illustrated History*. Hippocrene Books, Inc., 2008 ISBN 13: 978-0-7818-1196-5

This well-written story takes us from prehistoric times to the Louisiana Purchase, the Civil War, two world wars, the modern civil rights struggle, and into the 21st Century. It describes politics, culture, and prominent individuals who played major roles in Missouri history such as Meriwether Lewis, Harry Truman, Mark Twain, George Washington Carver, and many others such as Satchel Paige, Stan Musial, and Scott Joplin.

Powell, Betty F. *History of Mississippi County*. BEL Library Service, P. O. Box 1506, HARRY S. TRUMAN STATION, INDEPENDENCE, MISSOURI 64055, 1975

This book focuses on the people of Mississippi County, Missouri and on topics such as Indian history, churches, earthquakes, agriculture, wars, transportation, and businesses. The 100-page appendix includes a biographical section and a 12-page list of city and county officials, some going back as far as 1845. The *History of Mississippi County* contains a treasure chest of facts, names, and photographs which should be fascinating to anyone who grew up in the area.

Roll, Jarod. *Spirit of Rebellion: Labor and Religion in the New Cotton South.* University of Illinois Press, 2010 ISBN 978-0-252-03519-7

This is a scholarly and well researched account of the struggles of black and white sharecroppers and day laborers in the Missouri Bootheel during the first half of the 20th century to survive the domination and exploitation by the social and political systems arrayed against them. Their courage and cohesion was buttressed by their evangelical Pentecostal faith as they sought to gain economic freedom, fairness, and respect. This book relates a fascinating history.

Stepenoff, Bonnie. *Thad Snow: A Life of Social Reform in the Missouri Bootheel.* University of Missouri Press, 2003. ISBN 0-8262-1496-7

This book describes the work of a courageous white land owner in the Missouri Bootheel who defied the wrath of his fellow planters by supporting downtrodden and desperately poor black and white sharecroppers during the Great Depression of the 1930s. Thad Snow was an independent minded activist with strong convictions about social justice, race, the futility of war, and the preservation of nature.

Stephan Themstrom, Ann Orlov & Oscar Handlin. *Harvard Encyclopedia of American Ethnic Groups.* Belhanys Press of Harvard University, 1980. ISBN 9780674375123

This is a comprehensive and detailed reference book with 120 contributors describing over one hundred ethnic groups living in the United States. These groups are defined by characteristics such as culture, race, ancestry, history, language, religion, and more. Some of these groups are indigenous to the United States and others originated in a wide variety of countries throughout the world. The book also contains essays about issues relating to ethnic groups such as immigration, conflict, discrimination, government, and definitions of what an ethnic group is.

Ward, Geoffrey C. *Unforgivable Blackness: The Rise and Fall of Jack Johnson.* Alfred A. Knopf, 2004. ISBN 13: 9780739455111

This book includes the violent aftermath of African American Jack Johnson's victory over white boxer James J. Jeffries for the World Heavyweight Boxing Championship on July 4, 1910. White people greatly resented Johnson's winning the championship, not only because he was black but also because of his flamboyant lifestyle.

During the night after the fight there were riots from Denver to Washington and from New Orleans to Chicago. Depending on the source, somewhere between 10 and 26 people were killed. Most of the fighting was between whites and the blacks who were celebrating Johnson's victory. This book was made into a PBS documentary film by Ken Burns in 2005.

Whittle, Dan. *Canalou: People, Culture, Bootheel Town.* Southeast Missouri State University Press, 2013. ISBN: 978-1-890551-08-7

*Canalou* is a collection of stories about the citizens of a very small southeast Missouri town built on swampland during the late 1800s. The area was then drained for agricultural use in the early 1900s. Through the years the community developed its own unique culture and heritage. This book consists of 89 vignettes between three and six pages which are filled with humor, nostalgia, and local history. Many of the stories are autobiographical.

# Biographical Sketches of Those Who Played Pivotal Roles in the Events Recorded in this Book

**Thomas Lee Arnold** (1922-2013) served in World War II as a medic in France after the "D-Day," Normandy invasion in 1944. He was with the 44$^{th}$ Infantry Division, the unit that escorted the famed rocket scientist Dr. Wernher von Braun to allied custody. He learned fluent French and received the Bronze Star during his military service. He was a 1943 graduate of Southeast Missouri Teachers College (now Southeast Missouri State University) in Cape Girardeau, Missouri. After the war, Arnold attended law school at the University of Missouri and graduated in 1948 on the GI Bill. Arnold then practiced law in Benton, the Scott County seat, and retired in 1994. Along with David Blanton he represented Joe Lester Slayton at his preliminary hearing on April 8, 1958. Arnold was involved in local and state Democratic causes. [*The Southeast Missourian* 4/28/13]

**David Edgar Blanton**, born 1908, the youngest of seven children, was independent minded and stood up for his principles. As a young man he worked for a clothing store and "borrowed" his way through the University of Missouri. When he returned to Sikeston, he became a prominent lawyer and was elected Scott County Prosecuting Attorney. At the time, David's father, "C. L." Blanton, editor of the *Sikeston Standard,* made it clear that he was opposed to civil rights for "coloreds" and was noncommittal concerning lynching. Readers sometimes called him the "polecat," (a skunk like animal.) These attitudes became a bone of contention between "C. L." and his sons. Incidentally, David Blanton introduced the author's father to his mother in 1936.

**Harry Cullen Blanton** (1891-1973) graduated third in his class of 258 from the Georgetown University Law School in 1914 and then became a prominent lawyer in Sikeston, Missouri for the next 50 years. He was appointed by President Franklin Roosevelt to the position of U. S. Attorney for the Eastern District of Missouri and served there from 1934 to 1947. In 1918 he was inducted into the Army and served briefly in an administrative capacity until the end of the War. He was active in the American Legion for 53 years. Blanton was a member of the Scott County Democratic Central Committee from 1920 to 1928 and was later elected to the Southeast Missouri Boy Scout Council. He was a member of the Kiwanis Club, Chamber of Commerce, Knights of Columbus, and the St. Francis Xavier Catholic Church. This brief note barely scratches the surface of Blanton's accomplishments and awards during his interesting and productive lifetime. He and his wife, Maureen, raised four sons and four daughters. [*The Sikeston Standard,* 3/20/73] [Special to the Missourian]

**Arthur Bruce** (1918-2010) was Sikeston Chief of Police from 1956 to 1973. He served on Governor Warren Hearnes' Crime Commission along with Senator John Danforth and was Harry Truman's personal bodyguard when he visited Southeast Missouri. Bruce served in the Army during peacetime from 1934 to 1937, but when World War II broke out he reenlisted and served from 1942 until 1946 to fight the Japanese in the South Pacific. Later in life he received a bronze plaque for his involvement and dedication to thousands of children in Little League programs. He coached and managed teams of all ages and was vice-president of the Girls Softball League. Arthur was elected to the SEMO Amateur Baseball Hall of Fame in 1984. He was a member of the First Baptist Church of Bertrand, Missouri. [*Southeast Missourian* 6/10/10]

**Marshall M. Craig** (1907-1998) graduated from the University of Missouri in 1930 and while there was captain of the Missouri Tigers basketball team. In 1930 he was selected first team All-American and in 1992 was inducted into the Missouri Basketball Hall of Fame. Marshall graduated from the University of Missouri Law School in 1932 and became an assistant U.S. attorney in St. Louis from 1937 to 1939. He later served as Mississippi County Prosecuting Attorney. He became a circuit judge of the 28th District in 1955 and served four terms until 1979 and was then appointed the first senior judge in Missouri.

Craig served eight years on the Sikeston Public Library board, served as secretary of the United Way of Sikeston, was a former director and vice chairman of the Sikeston Industrial Development Council, and a former member of the Sikeston Public Schools Advisory Council. He was a longtime member of the Sikeston and Charleston Lions Clubs and past commander of several American Legion Posts. He was a member of the First United Methodist Church where he had been a Sunday School teacher. He was also a member of the Masonic Lodge. Craig was an Eagle Scout and served as president of the SEMO Boy Scout Council and had been a worker for the Salvation Army. [*Southeast Missourian* 9/2/98]

**Robert A. Dempster** (1912-1995) was a philanthropist and civic leader in Sikeston, Missouri who practiced law there for 59 years, from 1934 to 1993. He graduated from the University of Missouri Law School in 1934 and during his senior year was elected city attorney of Sikeston. For many years he was a major benefactor of Southeast Missouri State University in Cape Girardeau and helped to establish the Southeast Missouri University Foundation. Over the years the foundation raised millions of dollars for the university. Dempster's wife, Lynn, was a member of the school's Board of Regents while Robert funded the construction of an auditorium and a Hall of Nursing. In addition to his gifts to Southeast Missouri State University, Dempster made many financial contributions to his alma mater, the University of Missouri in Columbia. A major portion of these contributions went to its law school of which he was a trustee. He was appointed to the University's Board of Curators in 1978 and during his time on the Board he was chairman of its finance committee. While in Sikeston Dempster helped to fund the construction of the Missouri Delta Medical Center's rehabilitation complex in Sikeston. He founded the Security National Bank of Sikeston and was appointed to the Board of Trustees of Scarritt College, a Methodist School in Nashville, Tennessee. In 1942 Dempster became an officer in the Navy and spent two and a half years on the Pacific Island of Okinawa during World War II. He left the Navy with the rank of lieutenant commander. Dempster was a member of the First United Methodist Church of Sikeston and was involved in the development of the Wesley United Methodist Church. [*The Southeast Missourian* 3/26/95]

**John Clint Dennis** (1917-2000) was the Scott County Missouri Sheriff from 1951 to 1976 during which he played a key role in the search and arrest of Lynn Wayne Hester and Joe Lester Slayton. In 1963 he was elected president of the Missouri Sheriff's Association. Dennis was a Marine during World War II and later served as a Missouri State Senator from 1976 to 1992. Dennis was appointed by Missouri Governor, James T. Blair, to the newly established Commission on Civil Rights. He died in Cape Girardeau, Missouri in 2000. [*Southeast Missourian,* 2000]

**(George) Weber Gilmore Sr.** (1919-2002) was born in Charleston, Missouri, graduated from Columbus University in Washington, DC, and practiced law in Sikeston, Missouri for 50 years during which, in the 1950s, he served as Scott County Prosecuting Attorney. In 1958 Gilmore prosecuted Lynn Wayne Hester for the murder of Johnny Malugen. Later he moved to Benton, Kentucky and continued to practice law until 1990. Weber Gilmore was a major in the U.S. Army in the Pacific during World War II and was awarded the Bronze Star. He was a member of the First Christian Church of Sikeston. [*Southeast Missourian,* 5/7/02]

**Roy Finley Hough** (1925-1979) joined the Army Air Corps and was ready to go into combat just as World War II ended. After an Honorable Discharge from the military, he studied law at Vanderbilt University and graduated in 1951. After he passed the Bar, he practiced law with Robert Dempster in Sikeston, Missouri for three years before going into private practice. In addition to law, Roy loved farming and owned a farm south of Morehouse, Missouri. He married Rosalie Marilyn Eddy in 1947 and had four children: Sandra Lee, John Edgar, David Finley, and Janet Ann. [source: David and Janet Hough 4/3/20]

**Chief Deputy Aubrey Michael** (1919-1989) was a self-employed farmer, sold real estate, and was the Scott County, Missouri Collector before becoming Chief Deputy Sheriff for the Scott County Sheriff's Department. He was an Army veteran, served in World War II, and was a member the American Legion where he was Commander of Post 369. He was also a member of the Shriners of St. Louis and the Benton United Methodist Church. [*Southeast Missourian* 3/14/89]

**Marshall Elmer "M.E." Montgomery** (1888-1976) was Scott County Prosecuting Attorney and Superintendent of Schools before becoming a Magistrate Judge, a position he held for many years. During his career he had been a schoolteacher in Morley (where he was born), Claypool, and DeSoto. He was a veteran of World War I, a member the American Legion, a 32nd degree Mason, a member of the Scottish Rite, and the First United Methodist Church of Sikeston. [*Southeast Missourian* 11/29/76]

**Eugene Marvin Munger** (1896-1968) had been a resident of the St. Louis suburb of Brentwood after having lived in Bloomfield, Benton, and Chaffee, Missouri. He graduated from the Chicago Law School in 1922 and practiced law in Southeast Missouri and St. Louis until he died in 1968. Munger was a veteran of World War I and by the end of it had achieved the rank of Captain. He served a term in the Missouri House of Representatives after having been elected in 1932.

**James Ernest Scott (**1893-1973) had been mayor of East Prairie, Missouri before he was elected Sheriff of Mississippi County in 1940. He served in that capacity until 1959 when he retired.

He was a well-known landowner in the area and a member of the Church of God. [*Southeast Missourian* 11/12/73]

# Index